Daily Science

GRADE 4

Writing: Barbara Price
Content Editing: Marilyn Evans
Pamela San Miguel
James Spears
Andrea Weiss
Wendy Zamora
Copy Editing: Cathy Harber
Laurie Westrich
Art Direction: Cheryl Puckett
Illustration: Greg Harris
Design/Production: Susan Bigger
Kathy Kopp

EMC 5014

Evan-Moor®
Helping Children Learn

Visit
teaching-standards.com
to view a correlation
of this book.
This is a free service.

Correlated to State and
Common Core State Standards

Congratulations on your purchase of some of the finest teaching materials in the world.

Photocopying the pages in this book is permitted for single-classroom use only. Making photocopies for additional classes or schools is prohibited.

Contents

What's in This Book?

Daily Science provides daily activity pages grouped into six units, called Big Ideas, that explore a wide range of topics based on the national standards for life, earth, and physical sciences. Every Big Idea includes five weekly lessons. The first four weeks each center around an engaging question that taps into students' natural curiosity about the world to develop essential concepts and content vocabulary. The fifth week of each unit offers a hands-on activity and review pages for assessment and extra practice.

The short 10- to 15-minute activities in *Daily Science* allow you to supplement your science instruction every day while developing reading comprehension and practicing content vocabulary.

Unit Introduction

Key science concepts and national science standards covered in the unit are indicated.

Background information is provided on the topic, giving you the knowledge you need to present the unit concepts confidently.

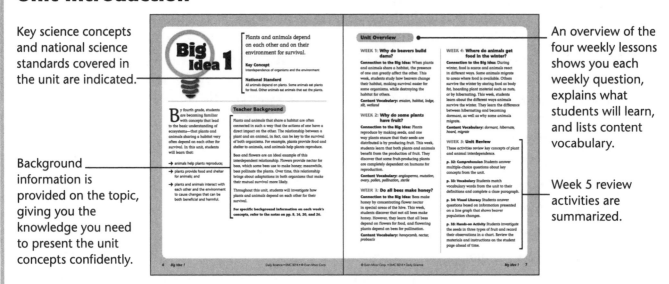

An overview of the four weekly lessons shows you each weekly question, explains what students will learn, and lists content vocabulary.

Week 5 review activities are summarized.

Weekly Lessons (Weeks 1–4)

Each week begins with a teacher page that provides additional background information specific to the weekly question.

Ideas are given for presenting the daily activity pages, including content vocabulary and materials needed for any demonstrations or group activities.

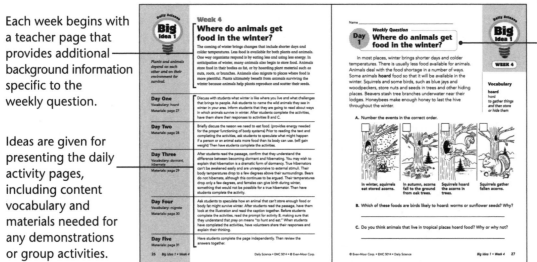

The student activity pages for Days 1–4 of each week use an inquiry-based model to help students answer the weekly question and understand fundamental concepts related to the Big Idea.

You may wish to have students complete the pages independently or collaboratively.

Weekly Lessons, continued

Each student page begins with a short introduction.

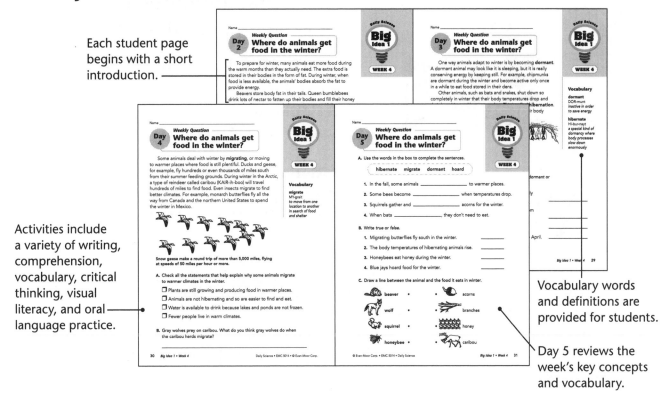

Activities include a variety of writing, comprehension, vocabulary, critical thinking, visual literacy, and oral language practice.

Vocabulary words and definitions are provided for students.

Day 5 reviews the week's key concepts and vocabulary.

Unit Review (Week 5)

Visual Literacy: Students practice skills such as labeling diagrams, reading captions, and sequencing steps in a process.

Hands-on Activity: Students participate in a hands-on learning experience.

Comprehension: Students review key concepts of the unit by answering literal and inferential comprehension questions.

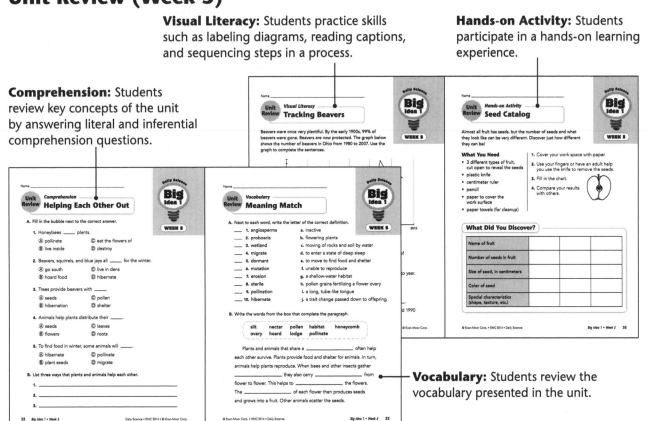

Vocabulary: Students review the vocabulary presented in the unit.

Big Idea 1

Plants and animals depend on each other and on their environment for survival.

Key Concept
Interdependence of organisms and the environment

National Standard
All animals depend on plants. Some animals eat plants for food. Other animals eat animals that eat the plants.

By fourth grade, students are becoming familiar with concepts that lead to the basic understanding of ecosystems—that plants and animals sharing a habitat very often depend on each other for survival. In this unit, students will learn that:

→ animals help plants reproduce;

→ plants provide food and shelter for animals; and

→ plants and animals interact with each other and the environment to cause changes that can be both beneficial and harmful.

Teacher Background

Plants and animals that share a habitat are often connected in such a way that the actions of one have a direct impact on the other. The relationship between a plant and an animal, in fact, can be key to the survival of both organisms. For example, plants provide food and shelter to animals, and animals help plants reproduce.

Bees and flowers are an ideal example of this interdependent relationship. Flowers provide nectar for bees, which some bees use to make honey; meanwhile, bees pollinate the plants. Over time, this relationship brings about adaptations in both organisms that make their mutual survival more likely.

Throughout this unit, students will investigate how plants and animals depend on each other for their survival.

For specific background information on each week's concepts, refer to the notes on pp. 8, 14, 20, and 26.

WEEK 1: Why do beavers build dams?

Connection to the Big Idea: When plants and animals share a habitat, the presence of one can greatly affect the other. This week, students study how beavers change their habitat, making survival easier for some organisms, while destroying the habitat for others.

Content Vocabulary: *erosion, habitat, lodge, silt, wetland*

WEEK 2: Why do some plants have fruit?

Connection to the Big Idea: Plants reproduce by making seeds, and one way plants ensure that their seeds are distributed is by producing fruit. This week, students learn that both plants and animals benefit from the production of fruit. They discover that some fruit-producing plants are completely dependent on humans for reproduction.

Content Vocabulary: *angiosperms, mutation, ovary, pollen, pollination, sterile*

WEEK 3: Do all bees make honey?

Connection to the Big Idea: Bees make honey by concentrating flower nectar in special areas of the hive. This week, students discover that not all bees make honey. However, they learn that all bees depend on flowers for food, and flowering plants depend on bees for pollination.

Content Vocabulary: *honeycomb, nectar, proboscis*

WEEK 4: Where do animals get food in the winter?

Connection to the Big Idea: During winter, food is scarce and animals react in different ways. Some animals migrate to areas where food is available. Others survive the winter by storing food as body fat, hoarding plant material such as nuts, or by hibernating. This week, students learn about the different ways animals survive the winter. They learn the difference between hibernating and becoming dormant, as well as why some animals migrate.

Content Vocabulary: *dormant, hibernate, hoard, migrate*

WEEK 5: Unit Review

These activities review key concepts of plant and animal interdependence.

p. 32: Comprehension Students answer multiple-choice questions about key concepts from the unit.

p. 33: Vocabulary Students match vocabulary words from the unit to their definitions and complete a cloze paragraph.

p. 34: Visual Literacy Students answer questions based on information presented on a line graph that shows beaver population changes.

p. 35: Hands-on Activity Students investigate the seeds in three types of fruit and record their observations in a chart. Review the materials and instructions on the student page ahead of time.

Daily Science

Big Idea 1

Plants and animals depend on each other and on their environment for survival.

Week 1
Why do beavers build dams?

Beavers, like all animals, depend on their habitat for survival. However, few animals affect their habitat as profoundly as beavers do. Beavers build dams to block the water in streams and create deep ponds. These ponds protect beavers from predators and create space for beavers to store their food cache in the winter. However, beaver dams can cause floods, completely changing the habitat where they live.

Day One

Vocabulary: *habitat*

Materials: page 9; pictures of dams

Introduce the week by asking students what a *dam* is. Show pictures of dams of various sizes, made from concrete or earth. Tell students that they will learn about an amazing little animal that also builds dams. After introducing the vocabulary word, direct students' attention to the illustration and ask what they can tell about a beaver's habitat. Then have students read the passage and complete the activities. For the oral activity, pair students or discuss as a group.

Day Two

Vocabulary: *lodge*

Materials: page 10

After introducing the vocabulary word, ask students to find the lodge shown on the page. Then have students read the passage to learn specific information about a beaver lodge. After students complete the activities, discuss their responses to activity C.

Day Three

Materials: page 11

Review what students have learned on Days 1 and 2—that trees provide beavers with building material for their dams and lodges. Tell them that today they will read about another reason trees are important to beavers. After students have read the passage and studied the picture, some may wonder how beavers are able to breathe when the pond is frozen over. Explain that the lodge walls, although thick, are not airtight. For activity B, you may wish to compose a response as a group and have students copy it onto their pages.

Day Four

Vocabulary: *erosion, silt, wetland*

Materials: page 12

Before students complete activity A, you may wish to discuss the positive and negative effects of beavers on the environment. If appropriate, draw the chart on the board and have students suggest answers for you to fill in.

Day Five

Materials: page 13

Have students complete the page independently. Then review the answers together.

    Daily Science • EMC 5014 • © Evan-Moor Corp.

Name _____

Day 1

Weekly Question
Why do beavers build dams?

Beavers are brown, furry mammals that live in lakes and rivers. To survive in this type of **habitat**, beavers build dams. They use their large front teeth to cut down trees and then pile up the wood to block the flow of water. This causes deep ponds to form behind the dam. The pond behind the dam gives beavers a place to hide. Beavers can get away from danger by diving into the deep water. The pond also provides a place for beavers to live and to store their food.

Vocabulary

habitat
HAB-ih-tat
a place where a plant or an animal naturally lives

A. Read each sentence. Write *true* or *false*.

1. A beaver's habitat has trees and water. _____

2. Beaver dams allow streams to flow freely. _____

3. Beavers run into the forest for safety. _____

4. A beaver can cut down trees with its teeth. _____

B. Use information from the passage to complete the sentences.

1. Beaver _____ are made of sticks and logs.

2. Water behind a dam gets _____.

3. Deep water provides _____ for beavers.

 Talk

What animals live in your area? What are their habitats like?

Name _____

Day 2

Weekly Question

Why do beavers build dams?

Beavers live in **lodges** that they build in the middle of the ponds created by their dams. The lodges are made of mud, sticks, and logs. Beavers enter the lodge through an underwater entrance. The inside of the beaver lodge is small compared to the outside of the lodge because beavers need thick walls to protect them from other animals.

Vocabulary

lodge
lahj
the dome-shaped home that beavers build from mud, sticks, and logs

A. Look at the diagram of the lodge. Label the entrances. Then write a sentence that gives information about the walls.

_____

B. Use the words in the box to complete the sentences.

> entrance   pond   underwater   lodge

1. For safety, a beaver _____ is built with thick walls.

2. The _____ surrounding a beaver lodge is like a moat around a castle.

3. The _____ to the beaver lodge is _____.

C. Foxes, bobcats, and coyotes hunt beavers. Why might beavers live in water?

_____

Name _____

Day 3

Weekly Question
Why do beavers build dams?

Trees are an important part of a beaver's habitat. Not only do they provide wood for shelter, but they provide food. Beavers are plant eaters, and their diet includes bark, leaves, and roots. During the summer, beavers stash logs and branches in underwater piles near their lodges to save for the winter. This is another reason why a beaver pond must be deep. If it is not deep enough, the pond may freeze all the way to the bottom in winter and the beavers will not be able to swim to their food.

A. Check the box next to the caption that best describes the illustration.

☐ Trees are only important to beavers during the winter.

☐ Beavers use logs they gather in the summer as food during the winter.

☐ Without leafy trees, most beavers will not survive the winter.

B. Explain in your own words why beavers need trees.

_____

_____

Name _____

Weekly Question

Day 4

Why do beavers build dams?

Beavers cause changes to the environment that can be both positive and negative. Ponds built by beavers create new **wetland** habitats for fish, frogs, and water birds. These wetlands also help slow soil **erosion** and keep more water in the ground, which allows plants to grow.

Beavers, however, also destroy trees that are homes for birds and other animals. In addition, beaver dams slow the flow of water in streams and cause **silt** to build up. Dams can also flood the land behind them.

A. List two positive effects and two negative effects of beaver dams.

Positive Effects	Negative Effects

B. Use the vocabulary words to complete the sentences.

1. When _____ builds up, it can make streams shallower.

2. _____ is a problem for farmers because water carries away the soil they need to grow crops.

3. Two animals that live in a _____ are ducks and frogs.

Vocabulary

erosion
ee-ROH-zhun
the moving of rocks and soil by water or wind

silt
silt
small particles of soil deposited by water

wetland
WET-land
a habitat where shallow water covers most of the ground

Name _____

Day 5

Weekly Question

Why do beavers build dams?

Daily Science

Big Idea 1

WEEK 1

A. Write the word that answers each clue.

> lodge   habitat   erosion   wetland   silt

1. small bits of soil that settle at the bottom of a river or lake _____

2. the place where plants or animals live _____

3. a beaver's shelter _____

4. a place mostly covered in shallow water _____

5. the washing or blowing away of soil _____

B. Check all the reasons why beavers build dams.

☐ Dams trap fish for the beavers to eat.

☐ Dams create ponds that are deep enough not to freeze solid in winter.

☐ Dams provide a sturdy structure for beavers to live in.

☐ Dams create ponds that beavers can hide in.

C. Write *true* or *false*.

1. In winter, a beaver cannot use the underwater entrance. _____

2. Beaver dams have no effect on the environment. _____

3. Beaver lodges are protected by water. _____

4. Beavers cut down trees. _____

5. Beaver dams only help beavers. _____

Big Idea 1

Plants and animals depend on each other and on their environment for survival.

Week 2

Why do some plants have fruit?

Plants reproduce by making seeds, and one way plants ensure that their seeds are distributed is by producing fruit. Fruits are fleshy structures that contain the seeds of the plant. Fruit attracts animals. When animals eat the fruit, they end up helping the plant distribute its seeds. This happens when seeds pass unharmed through the animals' digestive systems or when foraging animals simply discard the part of the fruit that contains the seeds. In this way, both organisms benefit.

Day One

Vocabulary: *ovary, pollen, pollination*

Materials: page 15; flowers with visible pollen, such as lilies; facial tissues for cleanup

After introducing the vocabulary, pass around the flowers, asking students to touch a stamen and notice the clearly visible pollen. Show students a flower with petals removed and identify the ovary at the base of the flower. Have students guess what fruit the illustration on page 15 shows (pomegranate) by explaining that the fruit is red and full of juicy seeds. Compare parts of the illustration to the flower you brought in. Then have students complete the page.

Day Two

Vocabulary: *angiosperms*

Materials: page 16

Introduce the vocabulary word and have students read the passage. After students have completed the activities, discuss their answers to activity A. As a group, generate a list of angiosperms that students are familiar with. (e.g., dandelion, rose, daffodil, etc.) If you wish to extend the lesson, explain that to reproduce, ferns produce spores and pine trees produce cones instead of flowers.

Day Three

Materials: page 17; cut-up pieces of fruit with seeds showing

Before students read the passage, discuss with them what foods they eat that have seeds. Ask students whether they eat the seeds and, if not, what they do with the seeds. When students have completed the activities, discuss their answers to activity C and ask them if they have accidentally helped to distribute seeds.

Day Four

Vocabulary: *mutation, sterile*

Materials: page 18

Introduce the vocabulary. After students read the passage, mention that mutations are common in plants and that this is how we often get new kinds of fruits or flowers with unusual colors or a combination of colors. Then have students complete the activities. For activity B, you may wish to tell students that some fruits with seeds have a seedless variety. (watermelons, grapes, oranges, etc.)

Day Five

Materials: page 19

Have students complete the page independently. Then review the answers together.

Name _____

Day 1

Weekly Question
Why do some plants have fruit?

Do you think plants make fruit just for you to eat? Actually, the main reason plants make fruit is because the fruit contains seeds, and seeds are how plants reproduce. The process of making fruit begins with a flower. After a flower blooms, grains of **pollen**, which are from the male part of the flower, combine with the female cells in the flower's **ovary**. This process is called **pollination**, and as a result, seeds form. The flower's ovary enlarges to form a fruit that surrounds the seeds.

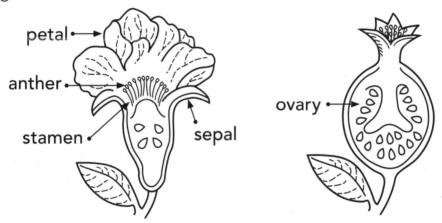

petal

anther

stamen

sepal

ovary

A. Number the steps in the correct order to show the process by which plants make fruit.

_____ Seeds form.

_____ A plant produces flowers.

_____ The plant's ovary grows into a fruit.

_____ Flowers are pollinated.

B. If animals ate flowers before they were pollinated, would this help or hurt a plant's ability to spread to new places? Explain your answer.

_____

_____

Vocabulary

ovary
OH-vuh-ree
the female part of a flower that contains the seeds formed after pollination

pollen
POL-un
a fine powder that comes from the male part of a flowering plant

pollination
POL-uh-NA-shun
the process by which grains of pollen combine with cells in the ovary to produce seeds

Name _____

Day 2

Weekly Question

Why do some plants have fruit?

Plants with flowers, called **angiosperms**, are very successful at reproducing. Today, angiosperms make up 90% of all plants on land. One reason for the success of angiosperms is the role flowers have in the production of fruit and seeds. Flowers attract bees and other pollinators. In turn, insects spread the pollen that is necessary to pollinate the plant and produce fruit.

Vocabulary

angiosperms
AN-jee-oh-SPERMS
plants that produce flowers

A. Circle the angiosperms. Then explain how you knew they were angiosperms.

  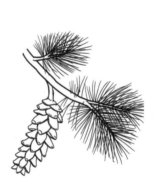 

_____

B. Use words from the passage to complete the sentences.

1. Most land plants are _____.

2. Pollen is necessary to _____ plants.

3. Flowers are a means to attract _____.

C. Describe the role of flowers in the reproduction of angiosperms.

_____

_____

Name _____

Daily Science

Big Idea 1

WEEK 2

Day 3

Weekly Question

Why do some plants have fruit?

Angiosperms benefit from animals not only when the animals spread the flower's pollen but also when they eat the plant's fruit. How is that? Animals help scatter a plant's seeds. Sometimes, animals just throw away the part of the fruit that contains the seeds. Other times, the seeds are eaten but passed through the animal's digestive system undamaged.

A. Use information from the passage to complete the sentences.

1. Plants make fruit to ensure that their _____ are distributed.

2. Seeds can pass through an animal's _____ system.

3. Animals help _____ seeds far and wide.

4. Animals often throw away the part of the _____ that has seeds.

B. Write *true* or *false*.

1. Birds scatter seeds. _____

2. Seeds are always destroyed if eaten. _____

3. Fruit protects seeds from being eaten. _____

C. Describe some of the ways humans help distribute seeds, either accidentally or on purpose.

_____

_____

Name _____

Day 4

Weekly Question
Why do some plants have fruit?

In nature, every fruit has seeds. So how is it that some fruits we get from the store, such as bananas and some grapes and oranges, don't have seeds? The first seedless fruits were probably caused by a natural **mutation**. Seedless bananas, for example, appeared about 8,000 years ago. Humans learned to grow the mutant banana plants by planting shoots that grow from the roots of a mature plant. All the bananas grown today are **sterile**. Without humans growing them, the seedless bananas we eat would disappear.

store-bought bananas

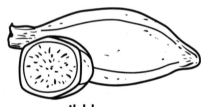
wild bananas

Vocabulary

mutation
myoo-TAY-shun
a change in a trait of an organism that is passed down to its offspring

sterile
STER-ul
unable to produce seeds that can grow into new plants

A. Use the vocabulary words to complete the sentences.

   1. All bananas grown today are _____ and don't have seeds.

   2. Scientists think a _____ caused the first seedless fruit.

B. Bananas are an example of a seedless fruit that couldn't exist without humans. Make a list of other seedless fruit you like to eat. Then list fruit that you wish *didn't* have seeds.

Seedless fruit that you like to eat	Fruit that you wish didn't have seeds

Name _____

Day 5

Weekly Question

Why do some plants have fruit?

Daily Science

Big Idea 1

WEEK 2

A. Use the words in the box to complete the sentences.

ovary	pollination	sterile
pollen	angiosperms	mutation

1. Seedless bananas were probably first caused by a _____.

2. Fruit is produced by a flower after _____.

3. Flowering plants are called _____.

4. If plants are _____, that means they can't produce seeds.

5. _____ grains combine with cells in the female

   plant's _____.

B. Coconuts are the giant seeds of coconut trees. Coconuts float in water, which allows the trees to spread to places where they have not grown before. Number the events below in the correct order to show how this happens.

_____ The coconut lands on the shore of a new island.

_____ The coconut falls from the tree.

_____ The coconut sprouts into a new coconut tree.

_____ Waves carry the coconut out to sea.

_____ Ocean currents carry the coconut for miles and miles.

C. Write at least one thing you have learned about plants and fruit that you didn't know before.

_____

Daily Science

Big Idea 1

Plants and animals depend on each other and on their environment for survival.

Do all bees make honey?

Nowhere is the interdependence of animals and plants clearer than in the partnership between flowers and bees. Many flowering plants require bees for pollination and attract them to their reproductive structures with scented and sugary nectar. Bees have special body parts for drinking and collecting nectar and pollen from flowers.

Not all bees produce abundant honey. In fact, certain species of bees produce no honey at all. However, all bees depend on flowers for food, and flowering plants depend on bees for pollination.

Day One

Vocabulary: *nectar, proboscis*

Materials: page 21

Invite students to share what they know about bees and any observations they've made about bees in nature. Before students read the passage and complete the activities, review or introduce the concept of *adaptation*—a change in a living thing that better enables it to survive in its environment.

Day Two

Vocabulary: *honeycomb*

Materials: page 22; honey from different sources; real honeycomb (available at natural food stores) or photos of honeycomb

Introduce the vocabulary word by passing around the honeycomb (or photos of honeycomb) for students to view. Elicit descriptions of the shape and, if using real honeycomb, the texture. Inform students that they will learn about honeycomb in today's reading. After students read the passage, look at the illustration and read the caption together. You may wish to do activity A as a group. Then direct students to do activity B independently.

Day Three

Materials: page 23

Before reading, have students guess the answer to the weekly question. Guide students' observations on activity A. (honeybee: smaller, less hair; bumblebee: larger, round, more hair) Then have students complete activity B independently.

Day Four

Materials: page 24; honeycomb (optional)

Before students do the first activity, examine the illustration of the beehive and read the labels. Explain the words *brood* (a group of young animals hatched at the same time) and *exclude* (to keep out). For the oral activity, you may wish to explain that there is concern about CCD because 90% of commercially grown crops in the U.S. depend on bees for pollination. Students may wish to research this further.

Day Five

Materials: page 25

Have students complete the page independently. Then review the answers together.

Name _____

Day 1

Weekly Question

Do all bees make honey?

If you look at the body of a bee, you'll notice some special features. One is the bee's long tongue, called a **proboscis**. A bee's proboscis works like a straw to suck up liquids. This is ideal for reaching **nectar** deep inside a flower.

You'll also notice that a bee is fuzzy. The fine hairs on a bee's body become covered in pollen when a bee visits flowers. The bee uses brushlike hairs on its hind legs to pack the pollen into compact bundles called pollen baskets. This is how honeybees get the nectar they need to make honey and gather the pollen used to feed the hive. In return, flowers are pollinated.

Vocabulary

nectar
NEK-ter
a sugary liquid produced by flowers

proboscis
pro-BAH-siss
the long, tube-like tongue of some insects

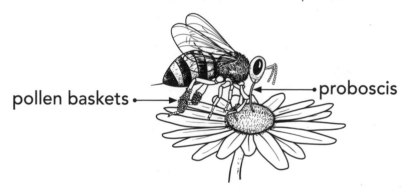

pollen baskets •   • proboscis

A. Use the vocabulary words to complete the sentence.

A bee's _____ works like a straw to

suck up _____ found inside flowers.

B. Explain how each of these adaptations helps a bee survive.

1. long tongue _____

_____

2. fuzzy body _____

_____

Name _____

Day 2

Weekly Question

Do all bees make honey?

A honeybee carries nectar back to the hive in a special sack in its body called a honey stomach. Back in the hive, the bee squirts the nectar from its honey stomach into waxy chambers called a **honeycomb**. Other bees then help dry out the nectar by fanning their wings over the honeycomb. Over time, the liquid becomes thicker and sweeter. It turns into honey, which provides food for honeybees all year long.

Vocabulary

honeycomb
HUN-ee-kohm
six-sided waxy chambers built by bees for storing honey and raising young

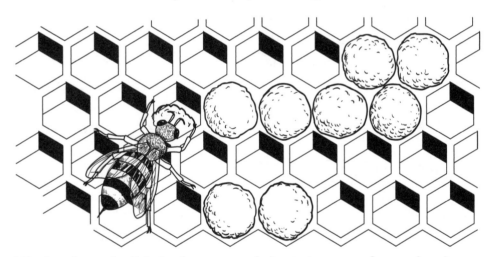

Worker bees build the honeycomb by using wax from glands on their bodies. They mold the wax with their mouths and feet.

A. Write one thing you learned from the caption above that you did not learn from the passage.

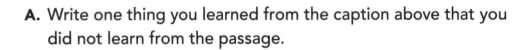

_____

B. Number the steps in the correct order to show how bees make honey.

____ Water evaporates from the nectar.

____ A bee carries nectar in its honey stomach back to the hive.

____ The nectar thickens into honey.

____ The bee squirts the nectar into a chamber of the honeycomb.

Name _____

Day 3

Weekly Question

Do all bees make honey?

Not all bees make honey. In fact, the word *honeybee* is used only for the type of bee that makes lots of honey. Bumblebees, for example, are different from honeybees. While bumblebees pollinate flowers and drink nectar like honeybees, they don't keep large hives with a honeycomb full of honey the way that honeybees do. Without a large supply of honey in storage for the winter months, most bumblebees die.

A. Look at the drawings of a honeybee and a bumblebee. On the lines below, compare and contrast the features of the bees.

honeybee

bumblebee

_____

_____

B. Check the characteristics that apply to each kind of bee.

	Honeybee	Bumblebee
Pollinates flowers		
Drinks nectar from flowers		
Produces large amounts of honey		
Creates honeycomb filled with honey		
Often dies in the winter		
Depends on flowers for survival		

Name _____

Do all bees make honey?

Although not all bees make honey, all bees pollinate flowers. The pollination of flowers by bees is very important to farming. Farmers will even hire beekeepers to bring beehives to the fields when it is time for the crops to be pollinated. For example, beekeepers bring hives to orchards when fruit trees are in blossom. Once the flowers are pollinated, fruit will grow on the trees. Then the bees can be moved to other crops.

This is a drawing of a beehive that many beekeepers use. Read the labels that name each part of the hive. Then, using the clues in the names, find the description below for each part. Write the letter of the description on the line.

_____ honey supers

_____ queen excluder

_____ brood boxes

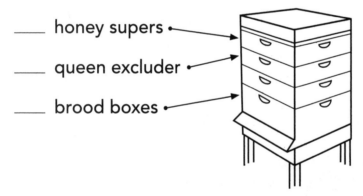

a. The spaces in this grid are too small for the queen bee to get through. It keeps the queen from laying eggs in the honeycomb.

b. Inside these boxes are hanging frames where the bees can build honeycomb and make honey.

c. This is where the queen lays eggs and the larval bees are fed by worker bees.

Since 2006, beekeepers are reporting that a larger than usual number of bees are disappearing. This problem is called Colony Collapse Disorder (CCD). Why do you think CCD has scientists and farmers concerned?

Name _____

Day 5

Weekly Question

Do all bees make honey?

A. Next to each word, write the letter of the correct definition.

_____ **1.** nectar   **a.** sweet liquid in flowers

_____ **2.** honeycomb   **b.** tube-like tongue

_____ **3.** proboscis   **c.** chambers bees make to store honey

B. Number the steps in the correct order to describe how bees collect pollen and nectar to feed the hive and, in the process, help plants to reproduce.

_____ The bee returns to the hive and squirts nectar into the honeycomb.

_____ A bee leaves the hive in search of nectar and pollen.

_____ Bees in the hive turn the nectar into honey.

_____ As the bee collects nectar from flowers, its fuzzy body picks up pollen.

_____ The bees use the honey for food during the winter.

_____ The bee moves from flower to flower, leaving behind pollen that pollinates the flower.

C. List three things that bees do to help people and plants.

1. _____

2. _____

3. _____

D. What would you tell someone who claimed that all bees make honey?

_____

_____

Plants and animals depend on each other and on their environment for survival.

Week 4
Where do animals get food in the winter?

The coming of winter brings changes that include shorter days and colder temperatures. Less food is available for both plants and animals. One way organisms respond is by eating less and using less energy. In anticipation of winter, many animals also begin to store food. Animals store food in their bodies as fat, or by hoarding plant material such as nuts, roots, or branches. Animals also migrate to places where food is more plentiful. Plants ultimately benefit from animals surviving the winter because animals help plants reproduce and scatter their seeds.

Day One
Vocabulary: *hoard*

Materials: page 27

Discuss with students what winter is like where you live and what challenges that brings to people. Ask students to name the wild animals they see in winter in your area. Inform students that they are going to read about ways in which animals survive in winter. After students complete the activities, have them share their responses to activities B and C.

Day Two
Materials: page 28

Briefly discuss the reason we need to eat food. (provides energy needed for the proper functioning of body systems) Prior to reading the text and completing the activities, ask students to speculate what might happen if a person or an animal eats more food than its body can use. (will gain weight) Then have students complete the activities.

Day Three
Vocabulary: *dormant, hibernation*

Materials: page 29

After students read the passage, confirm that they understand the difference between becoming dormant and hibernating. You may wish to explain that hibernation is a dramatic form of dormancy. True hibernators can't be awakened easily and are unresponsive to external stimuli. Their body temperatures drop to a few degrees above their surroundings. Bears do not hibernate, although this continues to be argued. Their temperatures drop only a few degrees, and females can give birth during winter, something that would not be possible for a true hibernator. Then have students complete the activity.

Day Four
Vocabulary: *migrate*

Materials: page 30

Ask students to speculate how an animal that can't store enough food or body fat might survive winter. After students read the passage, have them look at the illustration and read the caption together. Before students complete the activities, read the prompt for activity B, making sure that they understand that *prey on* means "to hunt and eat." When students have completed the activities, have volunteers share their responses and explain their thinking.

Day Five
Materials: page 31

Have students complete the page independently. Then review the answers together.

Name _____

Day 1

Weekly Question
Where do animals get food in the winter?

In most places, winter brings shorter days and colder temperatures. There is usually less food available for animals. Animals deal with the food shortage in a number of ways. Some animals **hoard** food so that it will be available in the winter. Squirrels and some birds, such as blue jays and woodpeckers, store nuts and seeds in trees and other hiding places. Beavers stash tree branches underwater near their lodges. Honeybees make enough honey to last the hive throughout the winter.

Vocabulary

hoard
hord
to gather things and then store or hide them

A. Number the events in the correct order.

In winter, squirrels eat stored acorns.

In autumn, acorns fall to the ground from oak trees.

Squirrels hoard the acorns in trees.

Squirrels gather fallen acorns.

B. Which of these foods are birds likely to hoard: worms or sunflower seeds? Why?

_____

C. Do you think animals that live in tropical places hoard food? Why or why not?

_____

Name _____

Weekly Question

Day 2

Where do animals get food in the winter?

Daily Science

Big Idea 1

WEEK 4

To prepare for winter, many animals eat more food during the warm months than they actually need. The extra food is stored in their bodies in the form of fat. During winter, when food is less available, the animals' bodies absorb the fat to provide energy.

Beavers store body fat in their tails. Queen bumblebees drink lots of nectar to fatten up their bodies and fill their honey stomachs. Bears eat enough during summer and fall to survive without eating all winter, while they are in a deep sleep.

A. Check the box next to each statement that is true.

☐ Fat provides energy.

☐ Fat becomes food.

☐ All animals store fat in their tails.

☐ Body fat can be stored for later use.

B. Use information from the passage to complete the paragraph.

Many animals get ready for _____ by taking

in more _____ than their bodies need. The unused

food is stored as _____. At the beginning of winter,

these animals weigh _____ than they will in the

spring. Their bodies use the fat to provide _____

during the cold months.

Name _____

Day 3

Weekly Question
Where do animals get food in the winter?

One way animals adapt to winter is by becoming **dormant**. A dormant animal may look like it is sleeping, but it is really conserving energy by keeping still. For example, chipmunks are dormant during the winter and become active only once in a while to eat food stored in their dens.

Other animals, such as bats and snakes, shut down so completely in winter that their body temperatures drop and their breathing and heart rates slow. This is called **hibernation**. Bears do something similar to hibernating, but their body temperature doesn't drop as much. Still, bears are able to go for months without eating.

Vocabulary

dormant
DOR-munt
inactive in order to save energy

hibernation
HI-bur-NAY-shun
a special kind of dormancy where body processes slow down enormously

Write whether each clue describes an animal that is *dormant* or one that is *hibernating*.

1. This animal's body temperature dropped only a few degrees. _____

2. This animal's body temperature dropped from 100°F (38°C) to 39°F (4°C). _____

3. This animal could be easily awakened. _____

4. This animal did not move from December to April. _____

Name _____

Weekly Question
Where do animals get food in the winter?

Some animals deal with winter by **migrating**, or moving to warmer places where food is still plentiful. Ducks and geese, for example, fly hundreds or even thousands of miles south from their summer feeding grounds. During winter in the Arctic, a type of reindeer called caribou (KAIR-ih-boo) will travel hundreds of miles to find food. Even insects migrate to find better climates. For example, monarch butterflies fly all the way from Canada and the northern United States to spend the winter in Mexico.

Vocabulary

migrate
MY-grait
to move from one location to another in search of food and shelter

Snow geese make a round trip of more than 5,000 miles, flying at speeds of 50 miles per hour or more.

A. Check all the statements that help explain why some animals migrate to warmer climates in the winter.

☐ Plants are still growing and producing food in warmer places.

☐ Animals are not hibernating and so are easier to find and eat.

☐ Water is available to drink because lakes and ponds are not frozen.

☐ Fewer people live in warm climates.

B. Gray wolves prey on caribou. What do you think gray wolves do when the caribou herds migrate?

_____

Name _____

A. Use the words in the box to complete the sentences.

hibernate   migrate   dormant   hoard

1. In the fall, some animals _____ to warmer places.

2. Some bees become _____ when temperatures drop.

3. Squirrels gather and _____ acorns for the winter.

4. When bats _____, they don't need to eat.

B. Write *true* or *false*.

1. Migrating butterflies fly south in the winter.   _____

2. The body temperatures of hibernating animals rise.   _____

3. Honeybees eat honey during the winter.   _____

4. Blue jays hoard food for the winter.   _____

C. Draw a line between the animal and the food it eats in winter.

 beaver •   •   acorns

 wolf •   •  branches

 squirrel •   • 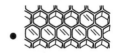 honey

 honeybee •   •  caribou

Unit Review *Comprehension*

Helping Each Other Out

A. Fill in the bubble next to the correct answer.

1. Honeybees _____ plants.

   Ⓐ pollinate   Ⓒ eat the flowers of

   Ⓑ live inside   Ⓓ destroy

2. Beavers, squirrels, and blue jays all _____ for the winter.

   Ⓐ go south   Ⓒ live in dens

   Ⓑ hoard food   Ⓓ hibernate

3. Trees provide beavers with _____.

   Ⓐ seeds   Ⓒ pollen

   Ⓑ hibernation   Ⓓ shelter

4. Animals help plants distribute their _____.

   Ⓐ seeds   Ⓒ leaves

   Ⓑ flowers   Ⓓ roots

5. To find food in winter, some animals will _____.

   Ⓐ hibernate   Ⓒ pollinate

   Ⓑ plant seeds   Ⓓ migrate

B. List three ways that plants and animals help each other.

1. _____

2. _____

3. _____

Name _____

Unit Review

Vocabulary
Meaning Match

Daily Science

Big Idea 1

WEEK 5

A. Next to each word, write the letter of the correct definition.

_____ **1.** angiosperms   **a.** inactive

_____ **2.** proboscis   **b.** flowering plants

_____ **3.** wetland   **c.** moving of rocks and soil by water

_____ **4.** migrate   **d.** a state of deep sleep

_____ **5.** dormant   **e.** to move to find food and shelter

_____ **6.** mutation   **f.** unable to reproduce

_____ **7.** erosion   **g.** a shallow-water habitat

_____ **8.** sterile   **h.** pollen grains fertilizing a flower ovary

_____ **9.** pollination   **i.** a long, tube-like tongue

_____ **10.** hibernation   **j.** a trait change passed down to offspring

B. Write the words from the box that complete the paragraph.

> **silt**   **nectar**   **pollen**   **habitat**   **honeycomb**
> **ovary**   **hoard**   **lodge**   **pollinate**

Plants and animals that share a _____ often help

each other survive. Plants provide food and shelter for animals. In turn,

animals help plants reproduce. When bees and other insects gather

_____, they also carry _____ from

flower to flower. This helps to _____ the flowers.

The _____ of each flower then produces seeds

and grows into a fruit. Other animals scatter the seeds.

Name _____

Unit Review

Visual Literacy

Tracking Beavers

Beavers were once very plentiful. By the early 1900s, 99% of beavers were gone. Beavers are now protected. The graph below shows the number of beavers in Ohio from 1980 to 2007. Use the graph to complete the sentences.

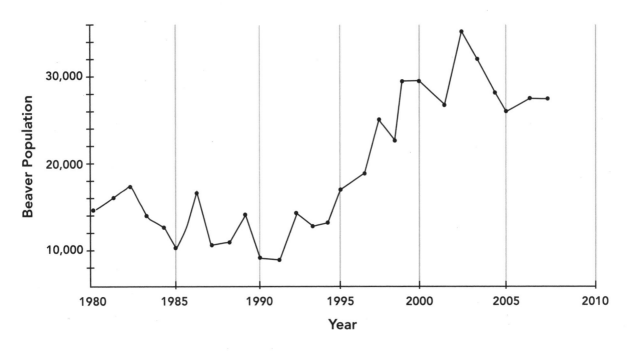

1. In 2005, there were _____ beavers compared with 1985.

   Ⓐ more than twice as many   Ⓒ half the number of

   Ⓑ the same number of   Ⓓ fewer

2. Overall, you can say that the number of beavers _____ year to year.

   Ⓐ always increases   Ⓒ never decreases

   Ⓑ stays the same   Ⓓ changes

3. The biggest increase in the beaver population occurred _____.

   Ⓐ between 1990 and 1995   Ⓒ between 1985 and 1990

   Ⓑ between 1995 and 2000   Ⓓ since 2005

Name _____

Unit Review

Hands-on Activity
Seed Catalog

Daily Science
Big Idea 1

WEEK 5

Almost all fruit has seeds, but the number of seeds and what they look like can be very different. Discover just how different they can be!

What You Need

- 3 different types of fruit, cut open to reveal the seeds
- plastic knife
- centimeter ruler
- pencil
- paper to cover the work surface
- paper towels (for cleanup)

1. Cover your work space with paper.

2. Use your fingers or have an adult help you use the knife to remove the seeds from each fruit.

3. Fill in the chart.

4. Compare your results for each fruit.

What Did You Discover?

	Fruit 1	Fruit 2	Fruit 3
Name of fruit			
Number of seeds in fruit			
Size of seed, in centimeters			
Color of seed			
Special characteristics (shape, texture, etc.)			

Big Idea 2

Most microorganisms do not cause disease, and many are beneficial.

Key Concepts
Bacteria, mold, and fungi

National Standard
All organisms cause changes in the environment where they live. Some of these changes are detrimental to the organism or other organisms, whereas others are beneficial.

By fourth grade, students know that bacteria and fungi are important decomposers. These microorganisms are responsible for recycling nutrients from dead plants and animals. In this unit, students will learn the following:

→ some bacteria are harmful to humans, many are helpful, and almost all are essential for life on Earth;

→ fungi, such as mold and yeast, are other microorganisms that can have both helpful and harmful effects;

→ as decomposers, bacteria can cause tooth decay; and

→ bacteria and molds in food play a role in the environment.

Teacher Background

Microorganisms are part of our everyday life. Some students may believe that all so-called "germs" are bad, when, in fact, the effects of microorganisms can be beneficial as well as harmful. Humans harbor many different microorganisms in their bodies that help them absorb nutrients from food. Certain bacteria, molds, and yeasts enhance our food and health.

Microorganisms are also decomposers, which means they break down dead plant matter and waste, converting them into nutrients that are useful to plants and animals. Without decomposers, organic material would not be properly recycled, and the world would be overrun with the remains of plants and animals.

For specific background information on each week's concepts, refer to the notes on pp. 38, 44, 50, and 56.

Unit Overview

WEEK 1: Why does garbage smell?

Connection to the Big Idea:
Microorganisms known as decomposers break down garbage and other raw organic material. This week, students are introduced to bacteria and fungi and learn how these microorganisms break down food.

Content Vocabulary: *absorb, bacteria, decomposers, fungus, mold*

WEEK 2: How do bacteria create cavities?

Connection to the Big Idea: In the process of decomposing, bacteria produce acids. This week, students learn that some bacteria in their mouths act on food left in the teeth. Students learn about the different parts of a tooth and how the acid from bacteria can destroy enamel and cause tooth decay.

Content Vocabulary: *acid, cavity, dentin, dissolve, enamel, fluoride, plaque, pulp*

WEEK 3: Are all germs bad?

Connection to the Big Idea: Infectious diseases can be caused by bacteria or viruses. Our immune system produces antibodies in response to infections. This week, students learn about viruses and bacteria and how they can be spread. They also learn that bacteria in our intestines are necessary for proper digestion and that scientists are discovering many new environmental uses for microorganisms.

Content Vocabulary: *antibodies, immune system, infectious, intestines, microscopic, viruses*

WEEK 4: Is it safe to eat moldy food?

Connection to the Big Idea: Some molds and another type of fungus, yeast, play an important role in food production. In addition, they are important in the creation of antibiotics. This week, students learn about other fungi and how these fungi can be used to create food and medicine.

Content Vocabulary: *antibiotic, microorganisms, nutritious, penicillin, yeast*

WEEK 5: Unit Review

You may choose to do these activities to review concepts of microorganisms.

p. 62: Comprehension Students answer multiple-choice questions about the key concepts of the unit.

p. 63: Vocabulary Students complete a matching activity to show that they understand unit vocabulary.

p. 64: Visual Literacy Students answer questions about information presented on a bar graph that shows tooth decay statistics.

p. 65: Hands-on Activity Students grow mold on four kinds of food and record their observations. Instructions and materials needed for the activity are listed on the student page.

Daily Science

Big Idea 2

Most microorganisms do not cause disease, and many are beneficial.

Week 1
Why does garbage smell?

Most students know that garbage—especially garbage that has been sitting around for a few days—smells! In this unit, students learn that the smell is caused by microorganisms decomposing waste. Bacteria and fungi are two common decomposers that consume waste. In the process, they break down large molecules into smaller molecules, some of which escape into the air. We notice these breakdown products as odors. Moisture and heat are factors that speed up the process of decomposition.

Day One

Vocabulary: *decomposers*

Materials: page 39

Introduce the week's question by asking students what they notice when they pass by a dumpster or a garbage can with the lid open. (bad smells) Tell students that they are going to learn about some organisms that are very important to our planet and, in the process, they will find out the reason that garbage smells. After students have read the passage and completed the activities, discuss their responses to activity C.

Day Two

Vocabulary: *absorb, bacteria*

Materials: page 40

After introducing the vocabulary words, activate students' prior knowledge by asking them what they know about bacteria. Take time to look at the illustrations showing the different kinds of bacteria. Then direct students to read the passage. Instruct students to complete the activities, and then discuss their answers to activity B.

Day Three

Vocabulary: *fungus, mold*

Materials: page 41

Introduce the vocabulary words. Point out that the plural of *fungus* is *fungi*. Then ask students to describe experiences with mold—where they have seen it, what it looked like, etc. After students read the passage, make sure they understand that fungi are not animals or plants but a separate classification of life. Point out the illustration and tell students that we see molds on the surface of things, such as this orange, but that the mold is spreading through this food to help break it down. Then instruct students to complete the activities. If students have not had much experience with analogies, you may want to do activity C together.

Day Four

Materials: page 42

Tell students that today they will find out the answer to the week's question. Direct students to read the passage and then, as a class, discuss why garbage smells. Next, instruct students to complete the activities. For the oral activity, you may wish to pair students or discuss the activity as a group.

Day Five

Materials: page 43

Have students complete the page independently. Then review the answers together.

    Daily Science • EMC 5014 • © Evan-Moor Corp.

Name _____

Day 1

Weekly Question

Why does garbage smell?

Everyone recognizes the smell of rotten garbage. It stinks! But that smell tells you that **decomposers** are at work. Decomposers are organisms that break down waste and dead matter, such as banana peels or wilted lettuce leaves. Decomposers are found everywhere, not just in trash cans. This is important because decomposers play a vital role in recycling nutrients and enriching the soil. If we didn't have decomposers, nutrients would never be reused, and the world would be filled with garbage!

Vocabulary

decomposers
DEE-kum-POH-zerz
organisms that break down and feed on waste and the remains of plants and animals

A. Name three effects that decomposers have when they break down waste.

1. _____

2. _____

3. _____

B. Write *true* or *false*.

1. Decomposers are important to the environment. _____

2. Decomposers are living creatures. _____

3. All decomposers live in trash cans and landfills. _____

C. Besides garbage cans, where else might you find decomposers?

_____

Name _____

Day 2

Weekly Question

Why does garbage smell?

Bacteria are the smallest decomposers, too small to see without a microscope, but they are the most numerous. There are many kinds of bacteria, and they live in every ecosystem on the planet, from oceans to deserts to your trash can.

Because bacteria are so small and simple, they don't have mouths with which to eat. Instead, bacteria release chemicals that break down matter into small parts that they can **absorb**.

Vocabulary

absorb
ab-SORB
to take in

bacteria
back-TEER-ee-uh
tiny one-celled organisms

spirilla
(spy-RIL-uh)

bacilli
(buh-SIL-eye)

cocci
(KOK-sy)

A. Fill in the chart with facts about bacteria.

Size of bacteria	
Where bacteria live	
How bacteria eat	

B. More bacteria live in your trash can than in your refrigerator. More bacteria live in a rainforest than on an iceberg. Write a sentence that explains how you think the cold affects bacteria.

_____

_____

Name _____

Day 3

Weekly Question

Why does garbage smell?

You can't see bacteria without a microscope, but you've probably seen a **fungus**, which is also an important decomposer. Mushrooms are a fungus, and so are molds. **Mold** appears as the patches of green, blue, or brown "fuzz" that you see on some rotting foods. You might think fungi are plants, but they are not. Plants make their own food, but fungi, like bacteria, can't make their own food. Instead, fungi absorb the food they need from whatever they are growing on.

Vocabulary

fungus
FUN-gus
an organism that absorbs nutrients from plants and dead plant material

mold
mold
a type of fungus

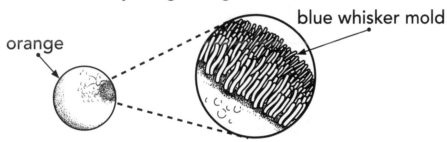
orange   blue whisker mold

A. Use words from the passage to complete the sentences.

1. One type of _____ is mushrooms.

2. _____ can be green, blue, or brown.

3. Both fungi and bacteria _____ the food they need.

B. A mushroom looks like a plant, but it isn't. What makes a mushroom different?

_____

_____

C. Complete the analogy.

Mold is to *fungus* as _____.

Ⓐ *dog* is to *cat*

Ⓒ *tree* is to *plant*

Ⓑ *bacteria* is to *garbage*

Ⓓ *mushroom* is to *mold*

Name _____

Day 4

Weekly Question
Why does garbage smell?

Garbage cans are ideal places to find decomposers because they are warm, wet, and full of food. The decomposers have everything they need to eat and grow. And unlike dishes and kitchen counters, garbage cans aren't cleaned with soap and water, so the decomposers aren't in danger of being killed.

When decomposers break down garbage into food for themselves, they produce substances that escape into the air as gas. We notice this gas as unpleasant odors. So keep the lid on your trash can. This will be better not only for you, but for the decomposers! It keeps their environment warm and wet.

A. Write *true* or *false*.

    1. Odors are produced when food decomposes. _____

    2. Decomposers grow best in cool, dry places. _____

    3. Decomposers turn garbage into larger particles. _____

B. Write whether each action described would make garbage smell *better* or *worse*.

    1. rinsing out food containers _____

    2. sealing rotting food in plastic bags _____

    3. putting the garbage in a warm place _____

Talk

Some people mix leaves, grass clippings, and leftover food to make a mixture that decomposes. This mixture, called compost, is used to enrich garden soil. Discuss with a partner some things gardeners can do to help the decomposers work.

Daily Science • EMC 5014 • © Evan-Moor Corp.

Name _____

Day 5

Weekly Question

Why does garbage smell?

A. Use the words in the box to complete the paragraph.

> fungus   absorb   mold   bacteria   decomposers

Decomposers such as _____ and

_____, which is a type of _____,

can be found everywhere, especially in your garbage can. When

garbage begins to smell, it means that _____

are breaking down large pieces of food into smaller particles.

The organisms can then _____ them as food.

B. Write *true* or *false*.

1. Bacteria are a kind of fungus.   _____

2. You would probably find more mold in a rainforest
   than in a desert.   _____

3. The world would be better off without decomposers.   _____

C. In your own words, explain why garbage smells.

_____

_____

Big Idea 2

Most microorganisms do not cause disease, and many are beneficial.

Week 2
How do bacteria create cavities?

Bacteria exist not only in the air, soil, and water, but also in our mouths. Students may be surprised to learn that there are 600 or more varieties of mouth bacteria! While most are either helpful or harmless, a strain of *Streptococcus*, called *S. mutans*, converts sucrose to lactic acid, which can erode tooth enamel. If unchecked, the growth of these plaque-forming bacteria in our mouths can cause tooth decay.

Day One

Vocabulary: *plaque*

Materials: page 45

Review the information that students have learned previously about bacteria. (e.g., they are microscopic, single-celled organisms; they are decomposers; they prefer warm, wet places to live) Introduce the lesson by asking students why someone's mouth is a good place for bacteria to live. (A mouth is warm, wet, and a place where food matter goes.) Introduce the vocabulary and then direct students to read the passage and complete the activities. Go over the answers together, recording responses to activity C so that students can check their predictions on Day 2.

Day Two

Vocabulary: *acid, dissolve*

Materials: page 46

Tell students that they will find out if their predictions about how bacteria cause decay are correct. After reading the passage, compare the information with what students predicted on Day 1. Then have students complete the activities and share their responses.

Day Three

Vocabulary: *cavity, dentin, enamel, pulp*

Materials: page 47

Ask students if they have ever had to see the dentist to have a cavity filled. As you introduce the vocabulary words for the parts of a tooth, instruct students to locate and label each part on the diagram in activity A. Then, while reading the passage, have students confirm each part on the diagram as they read about it. After students have completed the page, review the answers together.

Day Four

Vocabulary: *fluoride*

Materials: page 48

Introduce the vocabulary word and allow students to share what they already know about good dental care. After students have read the passage, complete the first activity together. For the oral activity, have students first share ideas with a partner, and then ask several students to report their ideas.

Day Five

Materials: page 49

Have students complete the page independently. Then review the answers together.

Daily Science • EMC 5014 • © Evan-Moor Corp.

Name _____

Day 1

Weekly Question

How do bacteria create cavities?

Bacteria are everywhere. In fact, you have about 10 times as many bacteria in your body as you have cells. And your mouth contains more bacteria than the human population of the world! Of the 600 or more types of bacteria in your mouth, most are helpful or at least harmless. One type of mouth bacteria, however, can damage your teeth if it grows out of control.

Bacteria are always multiplying on your teeth. Communities of bacteria combine with food debris to form a sticky, colorless coating called **plaque**. Dental plaque can contain billions of bacteria, and it is the first step in the process of tooth decay.

Vocabulary

plaque
plack
a sticky coating created by bacteria growing on teeth

A. Write *true* or *false*.

1. Bacteria in your body outnumber your cells 10 to one. _____

2. All the bacteria in our mouths are harmful. _____

3. A layer of plaque protects our teeth from tooth decay. _____

4. Plaque contains billions of bacteria. _____

5. Tooth decay causes plaque to form on your teeth. _____

B. How do you think bacteria cause tooth decay? Make a prediction.

_____

_____

Name _____

Day 2

Weekly Question

How do bacteria create cavities?

Daily Science

Big Idea 2

WEEK 2

Since bacteria eat the same food you do, you end up feeding mouth bacteria every time you eat and drink. Bacteria in our mouths thrive on sweet or starchy foods, such as soda, cookies, and potatoes.

As decomposers, bacteria work to break down the sugars in food into smaller substances that they can absorb. As bacteria break down and eat sugars, one of the substances they produce is **acid**. This acid can **dissolve** your teeth.

A. Use the words in the box to complete the paragraph.

> acid   bacteria   dissolve

Vocabulary

acid
AS-id
a substance produced by mouth bacteria

dissolve
dih-ZOLV
to break apart

Because _____ are living things, they

break down and consume food for energy. One thing that

bacteria produce during the process is _____.

It isn't as strong as other kinds of acid, but it can slowly

_____ your teeth if it isn't removed regularly.

B. Fill in the missing steps that explain how bacteria cause tooth decay.

| A person eats something sweet. | → | | → | Bacteria produce acid. | → | |

Daily Science • EMC 5014 • © Evan-Moor Corp.

Name _____

The outer layer of your teeth is made of **enamel**, which is pretty strong. But when your teeth are coated with plaque, the acid made by bacteria stays in contact with the enamel. Over time, it can dissolve the enamel. The result is a **cavity**. But tooth decay doesn't stop there. The next layer of a tooth is the **dentin**. If acid starts to dissolve the dentin, your tooth will start to hurt because the tooth **pulp** will be exposed. This is the part of the tooth that is alive and has the most feeling. If you don't stop tooth decay, you might get a serious bacterial infection!

A. Use information from the passage to label the parts of the tooth.

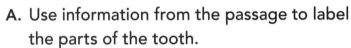

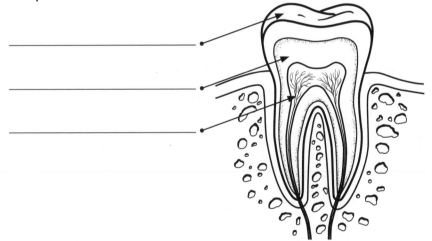

Vocabulary

cavity
KAV-ih-tee
a hole in a tooth

dentin
DEN-tin
the bony material that makes up most of the hard part of a tooth

enamel
ee-NAM-ul
a tooth's hard outer coating

pulp
pulp
the soft, living part of a tooth

B. Number the steps to show the order of the process of tooth decay.

_____ The tooth enamel begins to dissolve.

_____ Plaque traps the acid on your tooth.

_____ If the cavity dissolves the dentin, you will get a toothache.

_____ Bacteria produce acid when they eat sugars in your mouth.

_____ A hole, called a cavity, develops on the tooth.

Name _____

Day 4

Weekly Question

How do bacteria create cavities?

When we brush and floss our teeth, we remove the food that bacteria eat. We also remove some of the plaque where bacteria grow. In addition, we make our teeth stronger, because most toothpastes contain **fluoride**, a substance that strengthens enamel.

The best way to prevent cavities is to see a dentist regularly. A dentist removes hard-to-reach plaque on your teeth before a cavity gets started. If you do get a cavity, the dentist will drill out the decayed part of the tooth and then replace the cavity with a filling that is hard. The filling protects the tooth.

Vocabulary

fluoride
FLOR-ide
a substance added to water and toothpaste to help prevent tooth decay

The pictures show what happens when a cavity is filled. Write the letter of the correct caption for each picture.

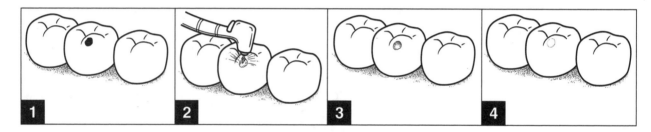

_____   _____   _____   _____

a. A dentist uses a tool to scrape away the enamel that has decayed.

b. The hole is filled with a material that becomes hard.

c. This is a tooth with a cavity.

d. Once the decay is removed, the hole in the tooth needs to be filled.

 Talk

Why is flossing so important in caring for your teeth?
Discuss this question with a partner.

Name _____

Day 5 *Weekly Question*
How do bacteria create cavities?

A. Use the words in the box to complete the paragraph.

> cavity   acid   dissolve   plaque

If you don't brush and floss after eating, bacteria in your mouth

form a film called _____ and release small amounts

of _____. If the plaque is not removed, the acid can

_____ your teeth's enamel. Then you have a _____.

B. Label the *dentin*, *enamel*, and *pulp*. Then complete the sentence.

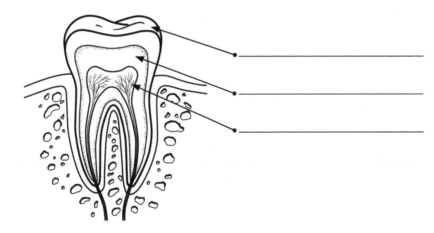

_____

_____

_____

The _____ is the part of the tooth that can become infected.

C. Write *true* or *false*.

1. Enamel is the living part of a tooth.   _____

2. Brushing kills bacteria in the mouth.   _____

3. Bacteria make acid that causes cavities.   _____

4. If you have plaque, you could get tooth decay.   _____

Daily Science

Big Idea 2

Most microorganisms do not cause disease, and many are beneficial.

Week 3
Are all germs bad?

Students should be familiar with the notion that germs cause illnesses such as colds or flu. This week, students learn that the germs that make us sick are comprised of bacteria and viruses. Our immune system creates antibodies that prevent viruses and harmful bacteria from reproducing. However, most bacteria are harmless, and some are necessary for our health. Our digestive system would not function properly without bacteria to decompose the food we eat. Bacteria are also helpful in many other ways, from creating energy to decomposing pollution. In fact, bacteria are so helpful that very few "germs" are actually bad.

Day One

Vocabulary: *infectious, microscopic, viruses*

Materials: page 51

Prior to the lesson, draw a chart on the board with these headings: *Types of Germs, Diseases,* and *Prevention.* Activate prior knowledge by asking students to share what they know about germs. After students have read the passage, help them complete the table by identifying bacteria and viruses as *germs,* colds and flu as diseases caused by germs, and hand-washing and covering sneezes as ways to prevent the spread of germs. After students complete the page, go over their answers together.

Day Two

Vocabulary: *antibodies, immune system*

Materials: page 52

Ask students if they have ever been around someone with a cold or the flu but didn't catch the person's illness. Tell students that they are going to read about how our bodies protect us from disease. Introduce the vocabulary; then direct students to read the passage and complete the activities. Go over the answers together to confirm students' understanding of the information.

Day Three

Vocabulary: *intestines*

Materials: page 53

After introducing the vocabulary and reading the passage, ask students if they were surprised to find out that their intestines contain bacteria. Then direct students to complete the activities.

Day Four

Materials: page 54

Tell students that they are going to learn about ways that bacteria are beneficial to the environment. If needed, explain what *toxic* means, as well as what sewage and water treatment plants are. After students read the passage, have them complete the activities. You may wish to have students work in small groups to complete activity B. Then have students share their descriptions of the experiment.

Day Five

Materials: page 55

Have students complete the page independently. Then review the answers together.

Name _____

Day 1

Weekly Question

Are all germs bad?

Have you ever had a cold or the flu? The "germs" that make you sick are usually bacteria or **viruses**. Bacteria and viruses are **microscopic**. Many germs can move easily from person to person. Germs on your hands can stay on the things you touch, such as doorknobs or keyboards. Germs can enter the air when you cough or sneeze. If a healthy person comes into contact with these germs, the germs can enter his or her body and make that person sick. Viruses and bacteria that cause disease are called **infectious** microorganisms.

bacteria

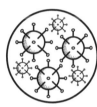
virus

Vocabulary

infectious
in-FEK-shus
able to cause or transmit disease

microscopic
MY-kro-SKAHP-ik
too small to be seen without a microscope

viruses
VI-russ-ehz
extremely tiny, infectious organisms

A. Write the letter to match each vocabulary word with its definition.

1. ____ infectious
    a. invisible to the naked eye

2. ____ viruses
    b. causing disease

3. ____ microscopic
    c. tiny disease-causing organisms

B. Number the steps in the correct order to show how the flu might spread from one person to another.

____ The person who breathes in the particles becomes sick with the flu.

____ A second person breathes in the virus particles through the nose.

____ Someone sneezes and spreads flu viruses into the air.

C. Write two characteristics that bacteria and viruses share.

1. _____
    2. _____

Name _____

Weekly Question

Are all germs bad?

Remember that viruses are tiny, infectious particles that cause disease. A virus must enter a plant cell or an animal cell to reproduce. When it enters the cell, it is infecting the plant or animal. Some viruses even infect bacteria cells! After a virus reproduces, the infected cell breaks open and the new viruses are released. These new viruses can infect more cells.

Luckily, our bodies have an **immune system** to protect us from viruses. The immune system makes **antibodies** that attach to viruses and keep them from entering our cells. Antibodies even keep some harmful bacteria from reproducing.

Vocabulary

antibodies
AN-tih-BOD-eez
substances produced by the immune system that stick to and destroy germs

immune system
ih-MYOON SIS-tum
a system in the body that defends against disease

A. Write the letter of the caption that describes each picture.

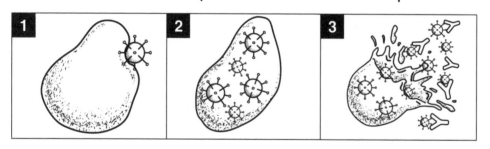

____   ____   ____

a. The virus reproduces inside the cell.

b. A virus enters a cell in the body.

c. When the viruses leave the cell, they are attacked by antibodies.

B. Use words from the passage to complete the sentences.

If it weren't for _____ created by our

_____, we would get sick more often. We would

be unprotected from harmful _____ that enter

the cells of our bodies and _____.

Name _____

Day 3

Weekly Question

Are all germs bad?

Not all bacteria cause disease. Some bacteria in air, water, and soil are important decomposers. They get their food by breaking down large particles of dead matter into nutrients that they can absorb.

You might be surprised to learn that bacteria do the same thing in our **intestines**! Our intestines contain billions of bacteria. These bacteria break down the food we eat, and cells in our body absorb the nutrients. In fact, without these bacteria, it would be very difficult for us to digest our food and get the nutrition we need to stay healthy.

Vocabulary

intestines
in-TES-tins
the part of the digestive system that absorbs nutrients from the food we eat

Use information from the passage to answer the questions.

1. What part do bacteria play in helping you stay healthy?

   _____

   _____

2. Antibiotics are medicines that kill bacteria. They are used to treat certain diseases, such as pneumonia and strep throat. How might taking antibiotics also have a negative effect on your body?

   _____

   _____

3. Yogurt is a food that is made by adding live bacteria to milk. Why might some people like to eat yogurt when they are taking antibiotics for an infection?

   _____

   _____

Name _____

Day 4

Weekly Question

Are all germs bad?

Scientists are finding many uses for bacteria. Since bacteria are such good decomposers, they can be used to clean up waste. One type of bacteria digests oil. People use it to repair damage from oil spills, both in the ocean and on roads. Other bacteria are good at breaking down toxic substances in sewage, so these bacteria are used in water treatment plants.

Scientists are also exploring ways to get bacteria to produce energy. Scientists have created simple fuel cells, which are like batteries, that use bacteria to convert garbage into electricity. These fuel cells may someday recycle waste into electricity during space flights.

So are all germs bad? Not at all. In fact, tiny bacteria may soon provide the solutions to some of Earth's biggest problems.

A. Use information from the passage to answer each question.

  1. How do bacteria clean up pollution? _____

_____

  2. How might bacteria help provide energy in the future? _____

_____

B. Suppose a scientist was studying bacteria in her lab to find out what the bacteria could help clean up. What do you think the scientist could do to learn what the bacteria were good for? How might the scientist set up her experiment?

_____

_____

_____

Name _____

Day 5

Weekly Question

Are all germs bad?

A. Next to each clue, write the letter of the word it describes.

____ **1.** These attack germs.

____ **2.** Food is digested here.

____ **3.** You can get a cold from these.

____ **4.** able to cause disease

____ **5.** When this is working well, you don't get sick.

a. infectious

b. viruses

c. intestines

d. antibodies

e. immune system

B. Write *true* or *false*.

1. Viruses infect cells and reproduce inside them.   _____

2. There are bacteria in your intestines.   _____

3. Viruses make antibodies.   _____

4. Bacteria can help with digestion.   _____

5. Germs block decomposers.   _____

6. Germs can be passed through the air.   _____

C. Describe how someone who is sick can spread his or her illness.

_____

_____

_____

_____

Daily Science

Big Idea 2

Most microorganisms do not cause disease, and many are beneficial.

Week 4
Is it safe to eat moldy food?

Students may not be familiar with the biology of mold, but they have likely seen mold's effects: mildew in carpets, mold on bathroom tiles, and moldy bread and cheese. These examples are likely to reinforce the idea that all molds are bad. In this week's activities, the benefits and uses of molds are explored. Molds are not only important decomposers, but they are also used in food preparation and in the creation of antibiotics.

Day One

Vocabulary:
microorganisms, nutritious

Materials: page 57; water, slice of whole wheat bread, self-closing plastic bag

Before introducing the vocabulary words and reading the passage, lightly sprinkle water on the piece of bread and seal it inside the plastic bag. Ask students what they think the bread will look like at the end of the week. Pose the following question: *Would you get sick if you ate the bread?* Record students' responses. Then have students read and complete the activities.

Day Two

Materials: page 58

After students have read the passage and completed the activities, go over the answers together, allowing students to share past experiences with moldy foods.

Day Three

Vocabulary: *yeast*

Materials: page 59; packet of dry yeast, glass of warm water, spoonful of sugar

Ask students if any of them have ever made or helped make bread. Explain that a necessary ingredient for making bread is yeast. Then dissolve the yeast and sugar in the warm water and tell students that the results will be examined at the end of the lesson. After completing the passage and the activities, show students the foam created by the multiplying yeast and ask them to explain what is happening based on the passage.

Day Four

Vocabulary: *antibiotic, penicillin*

Materials: page 60

Ask students if any of them have ever taken antibiotics when they were sick. Tell them they are going to read about the discovery of the first antibiotic medicine and learn what mold had to do with it. Introduce the vocabulary words, and then direct students to read the passage and complete the activities.

Day Five

Materials: page 61; bread from the beginning of the week

Have students complete the page independently. Then review the answers together. Invite students to examine the bread you stored in the bag on Day 1 and discuss the mold growing on it.

Name _____

Day 1

Weekly Question

Is it safe to eat moldy food?

Have you ever been about to eat a slice of bread or cheese when you noticed fuzzy green spots all over it? Yuck!

You can find mold almost anywhere, from spoiled food to bathroom walls. A patch of mold contains millions of **microorganisms**. These microorganisms are all around us, and when they come into contact with wet surfaces, they start to reproduce. Like all fungi, mold is a decomposer that breaks down substances in order to get nutrients. Sometimes, mold finds sources of nutrients that are surprising. You might not think your shower curtain is nutritious, but to mold it is good food!

Vocabulary

microorganisms
MY-kro-OR-guh-niz-emz
living organisms that are visible only through a microscope

nutritious
new-TRISH-us
full of nutrients

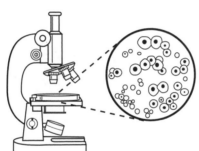

A patch of mold contains millions of microorganisms.

A. Use information from the passage to complete the sentences.

    1. The _____ that create mold reproduce when they come into contact with water.

    2. Mold can decompose many things, as long as there is water and a source of _____.

B. Make a check next to all the places where mold can grow.

    ____ clean, dry towel   ____ locker room

    ____ leaking water pipe   ____ hot oven

    ____ sealed jar of mayonnaise   ____ garbage can

Name _____

Day 2

Weekly Question

Is it safe to eat moldy food?

Certain molds are used to make some kinds of cheese. If you've ever eaten bleu cheese, you ate one of the *Penicillium* molds. The blue or green color inside the cheese is from mold! During the cheese-making process, either the mold is added to the milk, or the cheese is ripened in an area where there is a lot of the right kind of mold in the air.

Not all molds should be eaten, however. Even if the mold itself might not be harmful, it can contain bacteria that would make you sick. Some people cut the mold off the outside of the food and then eat the food, but this isn't a good idea either. Mold sends out threadlike roots that burrow into the foods they grow on, so mold you can't see may be inside the food. If your fruit or bread has mold on it, throw it out!

mold

mold roots

A. Write *true* or *false*.

1. You can't always see mold inside food. _____

2. Mold is allowed to grow in some cheeses on purpose. _____

3. All kinds of mold are all right to eat. _____

B. Answer the questions.

1. When is it safe to eat food that has mold? _____

_____

2. What is dangerous about moldy food, even if you remove the spots of mold?

_____

Name _____

Day 3

Weekly Question

Is it safe to eat moldy food?

Yeast is a common fungus that is used to make bread. Like most fungi, yeast grows best in warm, moist places. When yeast is added to flour and water, the tiny organisms start to grow and divide. Yeast gets food and water from the bread dough, and as the yeast organisms multiply, they produce carbon dioxide as waste. This gas makes the bread dough get puffy and rise. Bread dough can expand to twice its size in just over an hour. When the loaves of dough are baked in a hot oven, the yeast is killed, and the bread stops rising.

Vocabulary

yeast
yeest
a microscopic fungus used to make bread and other foods

 yeast cells

A. Number the sentences in the correct order to explain how yeast is used in bread making.

____ The gas bubbles are trapped in the dough, making it expand.

____ Yeast feeds on the dough and multiplies.

____ When the bread dough is baked, the yeast stops growing and the bread stops rising.

____ As yeast feeds, it produces carbon dioxide gas.

B. Complete the sentences.

1. Bread dough will not rise properly in a cold room because

_____.

2. Bread is light and fluffy because _____.

3. Bread does not keep rising while it is being baked because

_____.

Day 4

Weekly Question

Is it safe to eat moldy food?

Do you know the story of Alexander Fleming, the scientist who discovered **penicillin**? Dr. Fleming returned from a trip to find that a kind of mold had destroyed the bacteria he was using in an experiment. Dr. Fleming thought that maybe a chemical from the mold could destroy bacteria in people, too. In this way, he discovered the first **antibiotic** medicine. Today, molds are the source for antibiotics used to treat infections.

Alexander Fleming, Scottish biologist 1881–1955

Vocabulary

antibiotic
AN-tih-by-AH-tick
a medicine that stops bacteria from growing in the body

penicillin
PEN-ih-SILL-in
an antibiotic produced by mold

A. Write the vocabulary word that is described by each clue.

1. medicine that kills bacteria _____

2. the first antibiotic _____

3. penicillin is an example _____

4. made from a kind of mold _____

B. Fill in the bubble next to the answer that best completes each sentence.

1. Dr. Fleming had the idea for penicillin when _____.

   Ⓐ he left for a trip

   Ⓑ bacteria destroyed his lab

   Ⓒ he wanted to treat an infection

   Ⓓ the bacteria he was studying died

2. Dr. Fleming was a good scientist because he _____.

   Ⓐ took many trips

   Ⓑ realized the importance of the mold killing the bacteria

   Ⓒ invented mold and bacteria

   Ⓓ wanted to change the world with his experiments

Name _____

Day 5 *Weekly Question*
Is it safe to eat moldy food?

A. Use the words in the box to complete the paragraph.

> penicillin   nutritious   microorganisms
> yeast   fungus   antibiotic

Mold and _____ are each a type of

_____. A patch of mold can consist of millions

of _____. Mold can grow in carpets and on walls.

All it needs is water and a source of _____ food.

Alexander Fleming discovered the first _____

medicine when he found mold growing on his samples of bacteria.

Something in the mold had killed the bacteria. The substance

Dr. Fleming identified is now called _____, and it

is still used today to treat infections.

B. Write *true* or *false*.

1. Yeasts are microorganisms.   _____

2. Molds grow best where it is hot and dry.   _____

3. Molds are decomposers.   _____

4. Molds grow only in houses.   _____

5. Antibiotics kill bacteria.   _____

Name _____

Unit Review

Comprehension
Microorganisms

A. Fill in the bubble next to the correct answer.

1. Both _____ and _____ are a type of fungus.

   Ⓐ mold, viruses   Ⓒ viruses, yeast

   Ⓑ bacteria, mold   Ⓓ mushrooms, mold

2. What is the main job of our immune system?

   Ⓐ It protects us from illness.   Ⓒ It makes antibiotics.

   Ⓑ It helps us digest food.   Ⓓ It helps repair cavities.

3. Which of these is a product of bacteria that can damage teeth?

   Ⓐ pulp   Ⓒ acid

   Ⓑ dentin   Ⓓ enamel

4. Which decomposer is used to make antibiotics such as penicillin?

   Ⓐ bacteria   Ⓒ yeast

   Ⓑ mushroom   Ⓓ mold

5. Which of these is NOT part of a tooth?

   Ⓐ enamel   Ⓒ dentin

   Ⓑ plaque   Ⓓ pulp

B. Name two useful things that bacteria and fungi do.

   1. _____

   2. _____

Name _____

Unit Review

Vocabulary

Microscopic Match

Daily Science

Big Idea 2

WEEK 5

Next to each word, write the letter of the correct definition.

_____ **1.** decomposers

_____ **2.** absorb

_____ **3.** bacteria

_____ **4.** mold

_____ **5.** fungi

_____ **6.** plaque

_____ **7.** antibiotic

_____ **8.** acid

_____ **9.** dissolve

_____ **10.** cavity

_____ **11.** dentin

_____ **12.** enamel

_____ **13.** pulp

_____ **14.** infectious

_____ **15.** microscopic

_____ **16.** virus

_____ **17.** antibodies

_____ **18.** immune system

_____ **19.** intestines

_____ **20.** nutritious

_____ **21.** yeast

_____ **22.** microorganism

a. full of nutrients

b. able to cause disease

c. an organism that reproduces inside the cells of another life-form

d. a "fuzzy" kind of fungus

e. substances produced by the body to destroy germs

f. the living tissue of a tooth

g. a hole in a tooth caused by bacteria

h. a substance produced by bacteria

i. a fungus used to make bread

j. organisms that break down things into smaller parts for food

k. an organism, such as bacteria, that can be seen only under a microscope

l. the body parts where digestion happens

m. what the body uses to protect itself against illnesses

n. mushrooms, molds, and yeast

o. food and bacteria stuck to teeth

p. the middle layer of a tooth

q. single-celled decomposers

r. to break down completely

s. a medicine used to kill bacteria

t. a tooth's hard outer layer

u. too small to see without a microscope

v. to take in

Name _____

Unit Review

Visual Literacy
Away with Decay

Scientists study all kinds of things in order to better understand people's behavior and health. For example, scientists studied how many people in the United States had some sort of tooth decay between 1988 and 1994, and again between 1999 and 2002. The graph below shows the percentage of the U.S. population that had tooth decay during these two time periods.

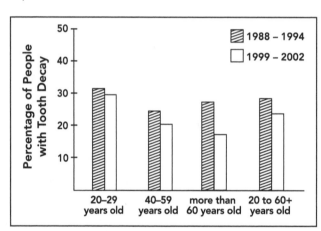

Use the graph to answer the questions.

1. Which age group had the highest percentage of people with tooth decay? _____

2. Which age group had the biggest DECREASE in the percentage of people with tooth decay? _____

3. Which age group had the LEAST amount of change in the percentage of people with tooth decay? _____

4. Overall, is tooth decay becoming a bigger or a smaller problem? How can you tell? _____

_____

Name _____

Hands-on Activity

Farming "Fuzz"

Mold is everywhere. The type of mold that grows depends on what the food source is. Try this experiment to see if you can grow different types of mold.

What You Need

- 4 sealable plastic bags or clear containers
- a piece of bread, an orange peel, a piece of carrot, and a piece of cheese
- water
- damp paper towels

1. Place each piece of food in a different bag or container, add a damp paper towel, and seal the bag or container.

2. Place the bags or containers somewhere warm, but not near anything too hot (such as a heater or oven).

3. Wait a week to see what grows. BUT BE CAREFUL. Some people are very allergic to mold, so you must keep the bags or containers closed at <u>all</u> times.

4. Look at your mold and fill in the chart below.

What Did You Discover?

	Bread mold	Orange peel mold	Carrot mold	Cheese mold
Color				
Size of moldy area				
Texture				

Which mold was the most interesting to you? Why?

_____

Big Idea 3

Both slow and rapid processes—from erosion to earthquakes—shape and reshape the Earth's surface.

Key Concept
Earth's surface is constantly changing.

National Standard
The surface of Earth changes. Some changes are due to slow processes, such as erosion and weathering, and some changes are due to rapid processes, such as landslides, volcanic eruptions, and earthquakes.

In this unit, students learn that the Earth's surface is shaped by slow processes—such as wind, water, and ice—and rapid processes—such as volcanic eruptions and earthquakes. In this unit, students will learn the following:

→ what created the Grand Canyon;

→ how the movement of glaciers created different landforms;

→ what happens when volcanoes erupt; and

→ why earthquakes occur.

Teacher Background

Earth's surface is enormously varied and continually changing. Mountains, valleys, islands, and canyons are some of the features that make up our planet's landscape. These landforms are created and affected by earthquakes, volcanoes, wind, water, and ice.

The emergence of landforms is also related to processes occurring deep within Earth's crust. Earthquakes and volcanoes are two expressions of these processes. Active volcanoes and earthquakes are constantly at work, creating new features and destroying old ones.

Once landforms emerge, they are shaped and reshaped by forces of weather and erosion. Recognizable geographic features, such as the Grand Canyon, were created over millions of years of weathering and erosion.

For specific background information on each week's concepts, refer to the notes on pp. 68, 74, 80, and 86.

Unit Overview

WEEK 1: How was the Grand Canyon formed?

Connection to the Big Idea: Students learn how the slow processes of weathering and erosion formed Arizona's Grand Canyon over a period of five to six million years. They learn that forces are still at work today, changing the canyon's features. Students then find out how humans affected the Grand Canyon ecosystem by building the Glen Canyon Dam.

Content Vocabulary: *channels, ecosystem, erosion, expanded, uplifted, weathering*

WEEK 2: Do glaciers really move?

Connection to the Big Idea: Students learn how glaciers form and what causes these "rivers of ice" to move. They also discover that in the past, glaciers carved out familiar landforms such as Yosemite Valley and the Great Lakes. Now, however, glaciers are retreating, which will have its own effects on the land in the future.

Content Vocabulary: *basin, glacier, meltwater, moraines, retreat*

WEEK 3: What makes a volcano erupt?

Connection to the Big Idea: To understand how volcanoes erupt, students first explore Earth's structure. They learn that lava comes from hot, soft rock in Earth's mantle, which turns into liquid magma as it nears the surface. Students discover that not all volcanic eruptions are explosive, and that steady flows over a long time can create landforms such as the Hawaiian Islands.

Content Vocabulary: *chamber, core, crust, debris, lava, magma, mantle, vent*

WEEK 4: What causes earthquakes?

Connection to the Big Idea: Earth's crust is not one piece but broken up into a dozen or so plates. Students learn that the motion of these plates as they move past, into, or away from each other along plate boundaries, or faults, is what causes earthquakes. Students read about the tool scientists use to measure the intensity of earthquakes and about the effects of earthquakes of varying magnitudes.

Content Vocabulary: *boundary, fault, magnitude, plates, seismometer*

WEEK 5: Unit Review

You may choose to do these activities to review the forces that shape Earth's surface.

p. 92: Comprehension Students answer multiple-choice questions about the key concepts of the unit.

p. 93: Vocabulary Students complete a crossword puzzle to show they understand unit vocabulary.

p. 94: Visual Literacy Students use an illustrated chart to gather information about three types of volcanoes.

p. 95: Hands-on Activity Students use "sandy" ice cubes to investigate the effect that glacial movement has on landforms. Review materials and instructions on the student page ahead of time.

Big Idea 3

Both slow and rapid processes—from erosion to earthquakes—shape and reshape Earth's surface.

Week 1
How was the Grand Canyon formed?

Plunging a mile deep into the desert landscape, Arizona's Grand Canyon exposes one of the most studied rock sequences in the world. Students discover that this spectacular natural landform is evidence that our planet has been, and continues to be, shaped by the geological processes of weathering, erosion, deposition, and uplift. This week, students learn that the walls of the Grand Canyon preserve a record of Earth's history going back two billion years. They also learn that in some sections of the canyon, human activity is changing geological processes at work today.

Day One

Vocabulary: *erosion, weathering*

Materials: page 69; pictures of the Grand Canyon, U.S. map

Show students pictures of the Grand Canyon and help students locate it on a map. Ask if anyone has visited the canyon and, if so, invite them to describe what they saw. Introduce the vocabulary and then have students read the passage. For activity B, remind students that *erosion* means rock is carried away, while *weathering* means that rock is broken down. Discuss the answers and make sure students understand each term.

Day Two

Vocabulary: *channels, uplifted*

Materials: page 70

When introducing the vocabulary, help students understand the meaning of *channels* by talking about what they have observed when they have seen rainwater flowing downhill. (It makes grooves, or channels, in the ground.) Then, as students read the passage, refer to each panel of the drawing that illustrates the text. You may also want to explain that the forces within Earth that caused uplifting are the same forces that cause earthquakes, which students will learn more about in Week 4 of this unit.

Day Three

Vocabulary: *expanded*

Materials: page 71

Review the terms *erosion* and *weathering* from Day 1. Instruct students to look for examples of these forces as they read the passage. Point out the illustrations below the passage and encourage students to refer to them as they read. During the oral activity, prompt students with examples you have seen if they are having difficulty thinking of examples on their own.

Day Four

Vocabulary: *ecosystem*

Materials: page 72

After introducing the vocabulary word, tell students that they will read about how humans have changed the Grand Canyon ecosystem. Have students read the passage and then read each scenario in the activity. If needed, discuss the problems as a class before students write their responses.

Day Five

Materials: page 73

Have students complete the page independently. Then review the answers together.

Name _____

Day 1

Weekly Question

How was the Grand Canyon formed?

One of Earth's most spectacular natural features is the mile-deep Grand Canyon in northern Arizona. It is also one of the best examples of **erosion**, where rock or earth is carried away, and of **weathering**, where rock is worn away or broken down. Looking from the rim of the canyon to the Colorado River below, visitors can see many layers of different kinds of rock. Some of the rocks are as much as two billion years old!

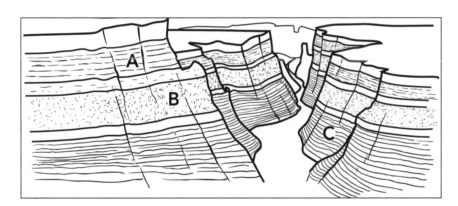

Vocabulary

erosion
ee-ROH-zhun
the moving of rocks and soil by water, wind, ice, or gravity

weathering
WETH-er-ing
the breaking down or wearing away of rocks by water or wind

A. Look at the drawing above. Write the letter of the layer that answers each question.

1. Which layer of rock was probably formed 2 billion years ago? _____

2. Which layer of rock was formed most recently? _____

B. Write whether each feature described below is due to *weathering* or *erosion*.

1. a river's bank becomes wider _____

2. canyon walls made wider by windblown sand _____

3. jagged rocks that have become smooth _____

4. a rock found a long way from others like it _____

Name _____

Weekly Question

Day 2

How was the Grand Canyon formed?

The Grand Canyon began forming five or six million years ago, after forces within Earth **uplifted** land and formed the Rocky Mountains. When rain fell, water ran down the sloping land and began to erode the soil, making **channels**. These channels eventually became the path for the Colorado River. Over millions of years, the Colorado River kept eroding the soil and carving out the canyon.

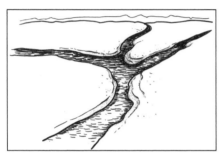

5 million years ago

Today

Vocabulary

channels
CHAN-ulz
cuts in the ground made by moving water, such as a river or stream

uplifted
UP-lift-id
pushed up

A. Number in order the events that formed the Grand Canyon.

_____ Uplift began forming mountains.

_____ As the channels got bigger and deeper, a river formed.

_____ Eventually, a deep canyon was formed with a river at the bottom.

_____ Water running off the land cut channels in the ground.

B. Check the box next to the thing in each pair that formed first.

1. ☐ Rocky Mountains **or** ☐ Colorado River

2. ☐ Colorado River **or** ☐ channels in the ground

C. Use the vocabulary words to complete the sentences.

1. Mountains are formed when land is _____.

2. Canyons start out as _____ carved by water.

Name _____

Weekly Question

Day 3

How was the Grand Canyon formed?

You know that erosion from the Colorado River was the major force that formed the Grand Canyon. But water also played a role in forming the canyon. Water seeped into cracks in the rocks and froze in the winter. When the water froze, it **expanded** and pushed the rocks apart. Then the pull of gravity caused sections of the canyon wall to collapse, making the canyon wider. Wind also shaped the canyon. Bits of sand, blown by wind, chipped away at the canyon walls and weathered the rock. All these forces are at work even today, continually changing the canyon.

Vocabulary

expanded
ek-SPAN-ded
got larger

A. Study the drawings. Underline the sentences in the passage that describe what the pictures show.

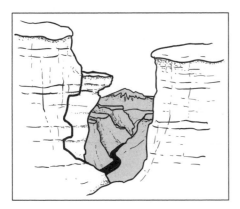

B. List the forces of erosion and weathering mentioned in the passage.

1. _____   3. _____

2. _____   4. _____

 Talk

What have you seen in nature that is the result of erosion or weathering? Think about places you have been or have seen in books or on television.

Name _____

Day 4

Weekly Question

How was the Grand Canyon formed?

Daily Science

Big Idea 3

WEEK 1

The Colorado River has always been important to the Grand Canyon **ecosystem**. When the river flooded, it helped native fish by carrying away rocks and sand that blocked parts of the river. Floodwaters deposited sand along riverbanks, building sandbars that became plant and animal habitats.

In 1963, water from the Colorado River was dammed up to create the Glen Canyon Dam. This meant that the natural flooding stopped. Scientists later realized that without flooding, the plants and animals living in the Grand Canyon suffered. Now the dam is occasionally opened to release a lot of water. This is done to preserve the ecosystem in the Grand Canyon.

Vocabulary

ecosystem
EE-koh-SIS-tum
a community of plants and animals and the physical environment in which they live

Below are two problems created by the Glen Canyon Dam. Explain how flooding might solve each problem.

1. The saltcedar is a shrub that, if left undisturbed, grows so thick that it stops other plants from growing. Saltcedar also traps salts from the soil and water, making the area around the shrub too salty for freshwater fish and amphibians to live.

saltcedar

_____

_____

2. The razorback sucker is a fish that lays its eggs in sandbars. It gets most of its food from riverbeds that have been churned up by a lot of flowing water. This fish is currently endangered because it cannot find enough food or places to reproduce.

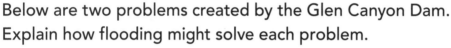

razorback sucker

_____

_____

Name _____

Day 5

Weekly Question

How was the Grand Canyon formed?

A. Use the words in the box to complete the sentences.

> erosion   channels   expanded
>
> uplifted   ecosystems   weathering

1. Rainwater can carve _____ in the soil.

2. Mountains form when the land is _____.

3. Soil being washed away is an example of _____.

4. Blowing sand can cause _____ of rock.

5. In _____, plants and animals interact with each other.

6. Over millions of years, the Grand Canyon _____.

B. Fill in the bubble next to the correct answer.

1. If you found a very young rock at the bottom of the Grand Canyon, what would be the most likely way that it got there?

   Ⓐ The rock was uplifted from below.   Ⓒ The rock was from a glacier.

   Ⓑ The rock fell from the cliff above.   Ⓓ Animals brought the rock there.

2. Over time, erosion and weathering can cause canyons to become _____.

   Ⓐ deeper and narrower   Ⓒ deeper and wider

   Ⓑ wider and shallower   Ⓓ shallower and narrower

C. Summarize how Glen Canyon Dam has affected the Grand Canyon ecosystem.

_____

_____

Daily Science

Big Idea 3

Both slow and rapid processes—from erosion to earthquakes—shape and reshape Earth's surface.

Week 2
Do glaciers really move?

This week, students learn that glaciers are not huge, stationary masses, but slow-moving rivers of ice that grind away rock, carve valleys, and create lakes. Glaciers move slowly, reacting to gravity and intense pressure that cause them to spread out and move. Today, glaciers are melting faster than they are growing due to the fact that Earth is warming. Scientists study glaciers to understand how Earth's climate changed in the past and how it might change again.

Day One

Vocabulary: *glacier*

Materials: page 75; photographs of glaciers

After introducing the vocabulary word, show students photos of glaciers from around the world. List words that describe the glaciers. (icy, white, chunky, like rivers, dark streaks, etc.) Ask students to speculate where the ice comes from. Then have students read the passage to find out. Before students complete the activities, confirm that they understand the meaning of *dense* (tightly packed, thick). Ask, *Which is denser, fluffy snow or ice?*

Day Two

Vocabulary: *meltwater*

Materials: page 76

Tell students that the passage they are about to read will answer the week's question. Then have a volunteer read the first two sentences aloud. Introduce the vocabulary word and direct students to read the remainder of the passage to find out what meltwater has to do with glaciers moving. You may wish to do the activity together to make sure students understand the two causes of glacial movement.

Day Three

Vocabulary: *basin, moraines*

Materials: page 77; map of the U.S.

Tell students that about 15,000 years ago, glaciers covered all of what is now Canada and the northern United States. These glaciers created many of the landforms we know today. Introduce the vocabulary and have students read the passage. Help students find Yosemite Valley and the Great Lakes on the map. Then have them complete the activities.

Day Four

Vocabulary: *retreat*

Materials: page 78; photos of glaciers (optional)

If possible, share photos of retreating glaciers, such as the Boulder Glacier, Easton Glacier, or Grinnell Glacier. Then have students read the passage and complete the first activity. For the oral activity, consider having small groups discuss the question and share their ideas with the class. Then provide the answers: According to scientists, if all of the Antarctic ice melted, sea levels would rise 180 feet (55 meters). If all the ice covering Greenland melted, sea levels would rise 23 feet (7 meters). Scientists are not sure how likely it is that all of Earth's ice will melt. However, even a three-foot rise in sea level would flood many coastal areas around the world.

Day Five

Materials: page 79

Have students complete the page independently. Then review the answers together.

Daily Science • EMC 5014 • © Evan-Moor Corp.

Name _____

Day 1

Weekly Question

Do glaciers really move?

Have you ever seen pictures of a snow-topped mountain? If so, you may also have been looking at a **glacier**. Glaciers are large sheets of ice that form in places where more snow falls than melts. As layers of snow build upon one another, the weight from a top layer pushes down on the layers beneath it. This pressure turns the snow to ice, like when you squeeze fluffy snow into a hard snowball.

Because glaciers form slowly, we can find them only in places that are cold year-round. Places like Greenland, Antarctica, and the tops of mountain ranges are good places for glaciers to form.

Vocabulary

glacier
GLAY-shur
a large, slow-moving mass of ice

← glacier

A. Write the two qualities that a place must have in order for a glacier to form there.

1. _____

2. _____

B. Write *true* or *false*.

1. Glaciers are made from many layers of ice. _____

2. Glaciers freeze in winter and melt completely every summer. _____

3. Glaciers are less dense than fresh snow. _____

4. Greenland and Antarctica have cold summers. _____

Name _____

Do glaciers really move?

Daily Science

Big Idea 3

WEEK 2

Glaciers might appear to stay in one place, but they are actually "rivers" of ice that flow downhill. Glaciers move in two main ways. One way a glacier moves is when it becomes so deep and heavy that it can't hold itself together. Gravity causes the ice to spread out, much like the way warm wax flows.

The second way glaciers move is by sliding. This happens because **meltwater** at the bottom of the glacier makes the ground wet and the glacier very slippery. Meltwater can come from melted ice that seeps through the glacier, or it can be created when extreme pressure from the ice above causes the ice at the bottom of the glacier to melt.

Vocabulary

meltwater
MELT-wah-tur
water that melts from a glacier

The pictures below show two ways a glacier can move. Using information from the passage, write a caption that describes each picture.

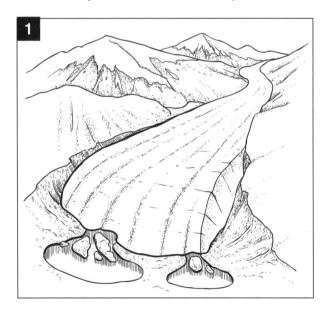

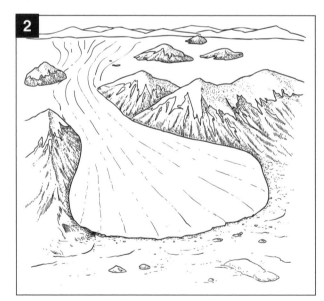

_____

_____

Name _____

Day 3

Weekly Question

Do glaciers really move?

Glaciers are the largest moving objects on Earth, scraping rocks and soil from their paths like giant bulldozers. We can see the effect of glaciers in many places. For example, California's Yosemite Valley was once filled by a glacier over 3,000 feet deep. This glacier carved a giant U-shaped valley in the rock and left behind ridges of dirt and gravel called **moraines**. In other places, erosion by glaciers resulted in the creation of lakes. The Great Lakes formed from **basins** scooped out by the passage of a glacier. When the ice melted, these basins filled with water.

A. Label each landform with the correct word from the passage.

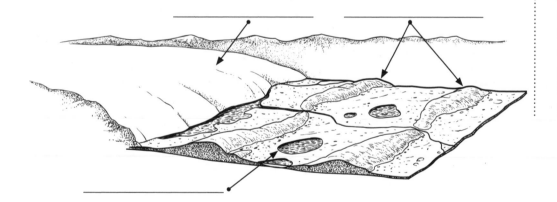

Vocabulary

basin
BA-sin
a large hole or depression in the ground that can contain water

moraines
mor-RAYNZ
ridges of loose rock and soil created by a glacier and left behind when the glacier melts

B. Use the vocabulary words to complete the sentences.

1. Animals looking for water might check small

_____ after a rainstorm.

2. Some _____ can become low hills.

3. A _____ contains a mixture of rocks and soil.

4. A bathtub is similar in shape to a _____.

Name _____

Do glaciers really move?

Today we live in a very warm period, and glaciers are on the move—backward! Most glaciers are melting faster than they are growing. This is called glacial **retreat**. Scientists study glacial retreat to understand how climate change will affect glaciers around the world. One way scientists do this is by comparing photographs of glaciers taken years apart. This tells scientists how much and how fast the ice is melting. In Canada's Glacier National Park, for example, most large glaciers are only a third of the size they were over 150 years ago.

Vocabulary

retreat
ree-TREET
movement backward

Look at the diagram of a glacier. The lines show how far the ice has retreated since 1850. Use the diagram to answer the questions.

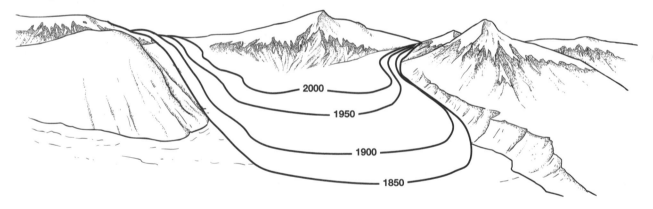

1. What span of time is represented by the diagram? _____

2. When was the glacier's rate of retreat the GREATEST? _____

3. When was the glacier's rate of retreat the SMALLEST? _____

 Talk

The continent of Antarctica and the island of Greenland are covered with glaciers. What might happen if these glaciers were to completely melt?

Name _____

Day 5

Weekly Question
Do glaciers really move?

A. Use the words in the box to complete the sentences.

> meltwater   glaciers   retreat   moraines   basins

1. A melting glacier leaves behind ridges of rock and gravel

    called _____.

2. One place to find large, moving _____ is in cold
    mountain areas.

3. Glaciers scoop out _____ that can later fill up
    with water.

4. The movement of some glaciers is helped by _____.

5. Climate change can affect the speed of a glacier's

    _____.

B. Write *true* or *false*.

1. Glaciers do not cause weathering or erosion.   _____

2. Gravity plays a role in the movement of glaciers.   _____

3. In the past, glaciers were more common.   _____

4. Yosemite Valley is an example of a moraine.   _____

C. Explain the role of pressure in how a glacier is formed.

_____

_____

Both slow and rapid processes—from erosion to earthquakes—shape and reshape Earth's surface.

Week 3
What makes a volcano erupt?

An erupting volcano is a dramatic example of the powerful forces that shape Earth's surface. Unlike wind, water, and ice, the processes that create volcanoes start deep within the planet. This week, students learn about Earth's layers and that volcanoes are created when hot, soft rock from Earth's mantle rises through cracks in the crust. As this material moves upward, it expands and melts, becoming magma. When volcanoes erupt, magma spills onto Earth's surface in the form of lava.

Day One

Vocabulary: *core, crust, mantle*

Materials: page 81; any fruit with a pit, knife

Cut the fruit you brought in and have volunteers use vocabulary words to compare the skin, flesh, and pit of the fruit to Earth's crust, mantle, and core. When students have completed activity C, have volunteers read aloud their answers and explain their thinking. Then explain that as Earth was forming billions of years ago, its heavier parts sank to the center, while its lighter parts rose to the surface.

Day Two

Vocabulary: *lava, magma*

Materials: page 82

Students may have difficulty understanding that while the rock in the mantle is soft, it is not liquid. Explain that there is no material on Earth's surface quite like the rock in the mantle, but it is similar to putty or toothpaste in that it holds its shape, but is pliable and can be formed. For activity B, consider first completing a Venn diagram or T-chart together. Then have students use the information to write their answers.

Day Three

Vocabulary: *vent*

Materials: page 83; pictures of the Hawaiian Islands

Before students read the passage, show the pictures of Hawaii and ask for theories about how Hawaii was formed. After students have finished reading the passage, explain that the volcanoes in this area of the world span more than 1,600 miles. When students have finished activity A, invite volunteers to share their responses.

Day Four

Vocabulary: *chamber, debris*

Materials: page 84

When introducing the vocabulary, consider asking students to list things they would consider to be *debris*. (e.g., trash, broken wood or glass, etc.) When students have read the passage and completed activity B, invite volunteers to share their responses.

Day Five

Materials: page 85

Have students complete the page independently. Then review the answers together.

Daily Science • EMC 5014 • © Evan-Moor Corp.

Name _____

Day 1

Weekly Question

What makes a volcano erupt?

To understand volcanoes, you must first understand Earth's layers. Earth's center is made of two parts, the inner and outer **core**. The core is made of liquid and solid metals. The next layer is the **mantle**. The mantle is solid and made of very hot, soft rock. The final layer is Earth's **crust**, which is the part we see. The crust is hard and brittle. Volcanoes form when hot liquid rock rises from the mantle through cracks in Earth's crust.

A. Use information from the passage to label Earth's *crust, inner core, outer core,* and *mantle.*

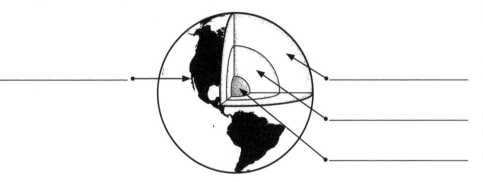

B. Use vocabulary words to complete the sentences.

1. Hot rock rises from Earth's _____

through cracks in Earth's _____.

2. Earth's _____ is hard and brittle,

while the _____ is soft and hot.

C. Which do you suppose is made from the densest, heaviest materials—the core, mantle, or crust? Explain your answer.

_____

_____

Vocabulary

core
koar
the center of Earth, made up of two parts: a liquid outer core and a solid inner core

crust
krust
the surface layer of Earth

mantle
MAN-tul
the layer of hot rock between Earth's crust and core

Name _____

Day 2

Weekly Question

What makes a volcano erupt?

Daily Science
Big Idea 3

WEEK 3

The hot, soft rock in Earth's mantle is always moving. Heavy rock sinks toward Earth's core, while lighter rock moves closer to the surface. As the lighter rock gets closer to the crust, there is less pressure pushing against it. The rock begins to expand and turns from a solid into liquid **magma**. When the magma flows from a volcano onto Earth's surface, we call it **lava**. As lava cools, it turns from a liquid back into a solid. Now it is hard rock, not soft the way it was in Earth's mantle.

Vocabulary

lava
LAH-vuh
magma that flows from a volcano

magma
MAG-muh
hot, liquid rock that comes from Earth's mantle

A. Write *true* or *false*.

1. Magma that flows from a volcano is called lava. _____

2. The heaviest rock in the mantle becomes lava. _____

3. The rock on Earth's surface is harder than the rock in Earth's mantle. _____

B. Compare and contrast rock in the mantle to lava. Name one way they are the same and one way they are different.

1. Same: _____

2. Different: _____

C. According to the passage, what is the difference between magma and lava?

_____

_____

Name _____

Day 3

Weekly Question

What makes a volcano erupt?

When volcanoes erupt, they can be either violent or quiet and steady. Quiet, steady eruptions are known as lava flows. Lava pours through a **vent** in the crust onto Earth's surface in a slow, constant stream. As it cools, it hardens and becomes rock. The Hawaiian Islands are the result of this kind of eruption. Over a long period of time, lava has been flowing out of the volcanoes directly into the Pacific Ocean. The lava cooled quickly and formed the rock that makes up the islands. In fact, the continuing eruptions mean that the Hawaiian Islands are still growing.

Vocabulary

vent
vent
an opening in a volcano through which lava can flow

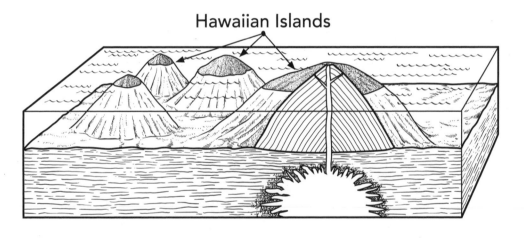

Hawaiian Islands

A. Summarize how volcanoes can form islands. Use *vent* in your summary.

_____

_____

B. Write *true* or *false*.

1. A lava flow is a violent eruption. _____

2. Rock made from lava cannot support large buildings. _____

3. Without volcanoes, the Hawaiian Islands would still grow. _____

Name _____

Day 4

Weekly Question
What makes a volcano erupt?

Daily Science
Big Idea 3

WEEK 3

Giant, exploding volcanoes are one of nature's most violent events. Most of these types of volcanoes are shaped like cones. And they were all formed by earlier eruptions of lava. These volcanoes have a deep **chamber** that fills with magma. A long tube runs from the chamber to a vent at the the top of the volcano, which is often made from solid rock. As magma fills the chamber, it releases gases. These gases build up under the layers of rock at the top of the volcano. Eventually, the pressure is so great that the volcano explodes, sending ash, gases, and other volcanic **debris** into the atmosphere.

Vocabulary

chamber
CHAYM-bur
a pocket under the volcano that fills with magma

debris
duh-BREE
small pieces of broken rock, lava, and other materials blown out during an eruption

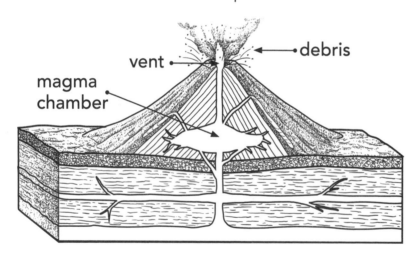

vent • debris
magma chamber

A. Write the vocabulary word that answers each clue.

1. This is hurled into the air during an eruption. _____

2. This fills with magma. _____

B. One way scientists tell that a volcano is ready to explode is by a bulge that sometimes forms near the top side of the volcano. Why do you think a bulge might form right before an eruption?

_____

Name _____

Day 5

Weekly Question

What makes a volcano erupt?

A. Use the words in the box to complete the sentences.

> lava   core   crust   vents
>
> debris   chamber   magma   mantle

1. _____ from the mantle that reaches Earth's

   surface is called _____.

2. The three layers of Earth are the _____,

   _____, and _____.

3. Hot rock from the mantle pours through _____
   in Earth's crust.

4. When volcanoes explode, they send ash, rock, and other

   _____ into the air.

5. Under some volcanoes there is a deep _____
   that fills with magma.

B. Write *true* or *false*.

1. Rocks in Earth's mantle change from a liquid
   to a solid as they rise toward the surface. _____

2. Volcanoes can create islands. _____

3. Rocks in the mantle are always moving. _____

4. Lava that cools becomes rock. _____

Daily Science

Big Idea 3

Both slow and rapid processes—from erosion to earthquakes—shape and reshape Earth's surface.

Week 4
What causes earthquakes?

Some of the most spectacular features on our planet—from the Himalaya Mountains to the Pacific and Atlantic oceans—have been created in association with earthquakes. In this week's activities, students will learn that earthquakes are caused by motions in the Earth's plates. While earthquakes can be destructive, they are also an expression of the dynamic forces within Earth that shape the planet on which we live.

Day One

Vocabulary: *plates*

Materials: page 87

Ask students to recall the layers of Earth they learned about in Week 3—*core*, *mantle*, and *crust*. Tell them that this week they will learn about earthquakes. Whereas volcanic activity involves both the mantle and the crust, earthquakes are generated in the crust. Before reading the passage, call students' attention to the illustration showing Earth's tectonic plates. Point out that the plates are not shaped like squares or triangles but are irregular. Before students complete the activities, take time to discuss the illustration and relate it to the passage.

Day Two

Vocabulary: *boundary, fault*

Materials: page 88

Activate prior knowledge by asking students to share what they know about earthquakes. Discuss the illustration before asking students to complete the activities.

Day Three

Materials: page 89; sheets of scrap paper

Students may have difficulty visualizing what happens when plates collide. After reading the passage, have students draw a line representing a fault across the middle of a sheet of paper. Direct them to put their hands on either side of the paper and push them together. The paper is pushed up in the middle just as Earth's crust is pushed up when plates collide. Also, tell students that when plates pull apart, it doesn't create a giant hole in the ground. Instead, volcanoes located at the boundaries usually send magma to Earth's surface.

Day Four

Vocabulary: *magnitude, seismometer*

Materials: page 90

On the board, write: *In May 2008, a 7.9 magnitude earthquake struck central China.* Ask a volunteer to read the statement. Then point out that scientists use numbers to indicate the strength of earthquakes. After reading the passage, ask students what they could say about the strength of a 7.9 earthquake. (e.g., buildings fall down) Before students complete the activity, read the chart together.

Day Five

Materials: page 91

Have students complete the page independently. Then review the answers together.

Name _____

Day 1

Daily Science

Big Idea 3

WEEK 4

Until the 1960s, scientists thought that Earth's crust was continuous and unbroken. Now they accept the theory that Earth's crust is broken into many irregularly shaped pieces called **plates**. There are eight large plates and a number of smaller ones. All the land and oceans lie on top of these plates. Beneath the plates is the hot, soft mantle. Because it is soft, the mantle moves, and it carries the plates along with it. So even though we don't feel it, the ground under our feet is moving all the time.

Vocabulary

plates
plaits
rigid sections of Earth's crust

A. Use the map to find where you live. Write the name of the plate you are on.

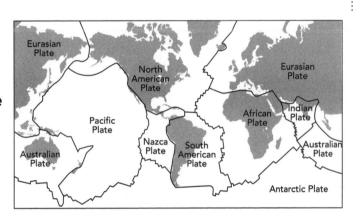

_____

B. Complete the analogy.

Earth's plates are to *mantle* as _____.

Ⓐ *raft* is to *water*   Ⓒ *hawk* is to *air*

Ⓑ *car* is to *road*   Ⓓ *rocket* is to *outer space*

C. Write *true* or *false*.

1. Earth's crust is broken into plates.   _____

2. Only continents lie on Earth's plates.   _____

3. The mantle is soft.   _____

Name _____

Day 2

Weekly Question

What causes earthquakes?

The movement of plates can be gradual or sudden. When plates move suddenly, an earthquake happens. Part of the ground may lift up several feet, or cracks in the earth may appear. The place where Earth's crust breaks is called a **fault**. A famous plate **boundary** is the San Andreas Fault in California. Here, one plate is moving north while the other moves south.

Vocabulary

boundary
BOWN-dree
border or edge

fault
fawlt
a break in Earth's crust where blocks of rock are moving in different directions

A. Use the diagram to answer the questions.

1. In which direction is this part of the Pacific Plate moving—

   north, south, east, or west? _____

2. Which cities would be affected by a major earthquake along

   the San Andreas Fault? _____

B. Use information from the passage to complete the sentences.

1. Earthquakes happen when _____ move suddenly.

2. A crack in the ground that runs for at least several miles is probably

   a _____.

Name _____

Day 3

Weekly Question

What causes earthquakes?

Plates move in all different directions. Plates sometimes slide past each other, like they do along the San Andreas Fault in California. Plates also collide, or run into each other. When plates collide, they cause powerful earthquakes and can even build mountains. The Himalaya Mountains in Asia are the result of two plates pushing together.

In other places, plates move apart from each other. This does not cause very strong earthquakes, but ocean basins are often created when two plates pull apart.

A. On the line below each picture, write whether the diagram shows plates *sliding past* each other, *colliding*, or *moving apart*.

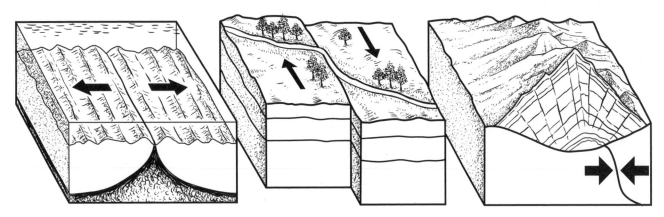

1. _____   2. _____   3. _____

B. Write *true* or *false*.

   1. Powerful earthquakes are generated as plates move apart.   _____

   2. Oceans are always created by plates colliding.   _____

   3. The San Andreas Fault is an example of mountain-building.   _____

   4. Plates sliding past each other can generate earthquakes.   _____

Name _____

Day 4

Weekly Question

What causes earthquakes?

Scientists study earthquakes with a tool called a **seismometer**, which records movements in the ground. In 1935, a scientist named Charles Richter invented a system of measuring earthquakes. This is called the Richter scale. An earthquake gets a number between 1 and 10 to describe its **magnitude**. A magnitude 1 earthquake is so weak that you can't feel it, while an 8.0 would knock you off your feet! Since scientists began using the Richter scale, the strongest earthquake ever recorded was a 9.5 in Chile in 1960.

Use the information in the chart to complete the sentences.

Richter Scale Magnitude	Average Number of Earthquakes	Earthquake Effects
2.0–2.9	1,300,000 per year	Not felt but are recorded on seismometers
3.0–3.9	130,000 per year	Barely noticeable; hanging objects may swing
4.0–4.9	13,000 per year	Most people notice them; buildings shake
5.0–5.9	1,300 per year	Everyone notices them; windows may break
6.0–6.9	134 per year	Walls may crack; chimneys may fall
7.0–7.9	18 per year	Ground cracks; weak buildings fall down
8.0–8.9	1 per year	Many buildings fall; bridges collapse
9.0–9.9	1 per 20 years	Complete devastation over a wide area
10.0+	Extremely rare	Never recorded

Vocabulary

magnitude
MAG-nuh-tood
a measure of the amount of energy released by an earthquake

seismometer
size-MAH-muh-ter
a tool that records movements in Earth's crust

1. Earthquakes of magnitude 9 happen at a rate of about _____ every _____ years.

2. Usually, an earthquake must be at least magnitude _____ to cause any buildings to collapse.

3. Most people notice earthquakes that are magnitude _____ or greater.

4. The number of earthquakes between a magnitude of 3.0 and 6.9 that happen every year is about _____.

Name _____

Day 5 *Weekly Question*
What causes earthquakes?

A. Use the words in the box to complete the sentences.

> magnitude   plates   fault
> boundaries   seismometer

1. Most earthquakes occur at plate _____.

2. When _____ collide, the land can be pushed up.

3. A _____ is a break in Earth's crust where rocks have moved.

4. A _____ is used to detect and record earthquakes.

5. The Richter scale measures the _____ of earthquakes on a scale of 1 to 10.

B. List the three ways plates can move to cause earthquakes.

1. _____

2. _____

3. _____

C. List three facts you have learned about Earth's plates.

1. _____

2. _____

3. _____

Name ______________________________

Unit Review

Comprehension

The Shaping of Earth

Daily Science

Big Idea 3

WEEK 5

A. Fill in the bubble next to the correct answer.

1. Which of the following is not associated with glaciers?

Ⓐ basins
Ⓑ plate boundaries
Ⓒ erosion
Ⓓ moraines

2. A feature of Earth's surface created by erosion is _____.

Ⓐ a mountain
Ⓑ an earthquake
Ⓒ a canyon
Ⓓ a volcano

3. As a result of weathering, a rock becomes _____.

Ⓐ taller
Ⓑ smaller
Ⓒ longer
Ⓓ larger

4. Which of the following is not the result of plate boundaries pushing against each other?

Ⓐ an ocean
Ⓑ a fault
Ⓒ a mountain
Ⓓ an earthquake

5. Lava from erupting volcanoes comes from Earth's _____.

Ⓐ core
Ⓑ mantle
Ⓒ ocean
Ⓓ crust

B. Write two things you learned about how Earth's surface changes.

1. ______________________________

2. ______________________________

Name _____

Unit Review *Vocabulary*

Puzzle It Out

Select from the list of vocabulary words to complete the puzzle.

basin	lava
boundary	magma
chamber	magnitude
channels	mantle
core	meltwater
crust	moraines
debris	plates
ecosystem	retreat
erosion	seismometer
expanded	uplifted
fault	vent
glacier	weathering

DOWN

1. large, rigid sections of Earth's crust
2. the moving of soil by water
3. this makes a glacier slippery
5. the top layer of Earth
8. hot, liquid rock from the mantle
9. ridges of gravel and rock
11. became larger

ACROSS

4. the layer of Earth between the crust and the core
6. pushed up
7. a break in Earth's crust
10. a process that breaks rocks into smaller pieces
12. this flows from a volcano
13. a hole in the ground that is created by a glacier
14. a slow-moving mass of ice

Name _____

Unit Review

Visual Literacy

Volcano Variety

Daily Science
Big Idea 3
WEEK 5

Study the chart to find out about three types of volcanoes.

Composite Volcano	Shield Volcano	Cinder Cone

• tall and steep-sided • formed from flows of sticky lava layered with other kinds of rocks • can explode violently	• huge and dome-shaped • formed from many layers of runny lava • erupts quietly and often	• small and cone-shaped • formed from blocks of cooled lava called cinders • lava erupts in sprays

Write the name of the type of volcano being described.

1. has flows of thick, sticky lava _____

2. forms the smallest type of volcano _____

3. erupts with quiet, steady flows of runny lava _____

4. explodes violently _____

5. formed from blocks of lava rock called cinders _____

6. has layers made from different kinds of rocks _____

Name _____

Unit Review

Hands-on Activity

Glacial Grind

In this investigation, you will look at the effect that glacial movement has on landforms. You will use "sandy" ice cubes as a model of a glacier that has pieces of rock in its ice.

What You Need

- ice cube tray
- water
- a few handfuls of clean sand
- aluminum foil
- plastic tub
- paper to cover the desk
- paper towels (for cleanup)

1. Make "sandy" ice cubes by sprinkling sand into an ice cube tray filled with water and freezing it overnight.

2. Smooth out a sheet of aluminum foil on the top of your desk.

3. Rub an ice cube across the sheet of foil.

4. Stack all the ice cubes on one side of a plastic tub and allow them to melt.

What Did You Discover?

1. What happened when you rubbed the ice cube across the foil?

   _____

2. What was left in the plastic tub after the ice cubes melted? What would this be called when a real glacier melts?

   _____

3. What did the experiment show you about the ways that glaciers change Earth's surface?

   _____

   _____

Big Idea 4

The properties of rocks and minerals reflect the process that formed them.

Key Concept
Rocks are composed of different minerals. They are made in distinct ways and have different properties.

National Standard
Earth materials are solid rocks and soils, water, and the gases of the atmosphere. The varied materials have different physical and chemical properties.

Students may not know that rocks are continuously created, destroyed, or otherwise altered by processes that are not directly observed. This unit focuses on how rocks are formed and how the properties of rocks reflect these processes. In this unit, students will learn the following:

→ how rocks are formed;

→ the types of rocks;

→ the properties of rocks;

→ the minerals found in rocks; and

→ the rock cycle.

Teacher Background

The appearance and properties of rocks depend on their mineral composition and the process that forms them. In this unit, students will learn what a mineral is and some of the different physical properties used to identify minerals. Students will also learn about the different types of rock and how they form, including rocks from outer space.

All rocks are made up of different minerals: natural, nonorganic solids with a crystalline structure. This means that the atoms in minerals have a regular, repeating structure.

Igneous rock forms from cooling magma, sedimentary rock forms from sediment, and metamorphic rock is igneous or sedimentary rock that has been changed by intense heat and pressure. Rocks from outer space either fall to Earth as meteorites or are collected by astronauts or probes. These lunar rocks share some minerals with rocks on Earth, but they also have their own unique properties.

For specific background information on each week's concepts, refer to the notes on pp. 98, 104, 110, and 116.

Unit Overview

WEEK 1: What's the difference between a rock and a mineral?

Connection to the Big Idea: Rocks are made from different minerals, depending on the processes that form them.

This week, students learn what a mineral is and the common physical properties used to identify minerals.

Content Vocabulary: *cleavage, color, crystalline, fracture, hardness, luster, minerals, streak*

WEEK 2: Where do rocks come from?

Connection to the Big Idea: The different kinds of rock—igneous, sedimentary, and metamorphic—have properties related to how each was formed.

This week, students learn about each type of rock, including some of the physical characteristics and how each type is formed. They then learn about the rock cycle.

Content Vocabulary: *cement, igneous, metamorphic, rock cycle, sediment, sedimentary*

WEEK 3: Are some rocks valuable?

Connection to the Big Idea: Minerals and some other natural resources, such as fossil fuels, are nonrenewable.

This week, students learn how fossil fuels and ores are gathered and used. They then learn that these resources are nonrenewable and must be conserved if they are to last.

Content Vocabulary: *carbon, conserve, extract, fossil fuels, metals, natural resources, ore, renewable*

WEEK 4: Do all rocks come from Earth?

Connection to the Big Idea: Rocks from space share some similarities with rocks on Earth, as well as some differences.

This week, students learn about three common sources for extraterrestrial rocks: asteroids, the Moon, and Mars. They learn how these rocks from space are similar to and different from rocks on Earth.

Content Vocabulary: *asteroids, extraterrestrial, lunar, maria, meteor, meteorite*

WEEK 5: Unit Review

You may choose to do these activities to review properties of rocks and minerals.

p. 122: Comprehension Students answer multiple-choice questions about key concepts from the unit.

p. 123: Vocabulary Students match key vocabulary words from the unit with their definitions.

p. 124: Visual Literacy Students use a chart listing different minerals and their properties to answer clues about the minerals.

p. 125: Hands-on Experiment Students learn more about sedimentary rocks by experimenting with chalk and vinegar. Review the materials and instructions on the student page ahead of time.

Big Idea 4

The properties of rocks and minerals reflect the process that formed them.

Week 1
What's the difference between a rock and a mineral?

Many students might confuse rocks and minerals as being the same thing. This week, students learn that a mineral is a single, inorganic substance made in nature that forms a solid and has a regular, repeating structure. Rocks are generally a mixture of several minerals. Minerals can be identified by the characteristics of color, streak, hardness, luster, and cleavage or fracture. If mineral samples can be obtained, it is helpful to have them available for students to inspect.

Day One

Vocabulary: *crystalline, minerals*

Materials: page 99; samples of minerals including salt, hand lenses

Activate prior knowledge by asking students to name the different contexts in which they have heard the word *minerals.* (in vitamins, in water, in relation to the ground or rocks, etc.) Introduce the vocabulary and use the illustration on the page to explain how something can be crystalline. Distribute hand lenses and some grains of salt for students to examine. After students have read the passage and finished the activities, reinforce the concept of how minerals form by asking: *If you wanted to make your own salt, would you need ocean water or magma?* (ocean water, because salt forms from evaporation)

Day Two

Vocabulary: *color, luster, streak*

Materials: page 100

Introduce the vocabulary and ask students if they have ever used chalk to draw. Explain that chalk is a mineral, and the lines you make with it are examples of its *streak,* one of the properties that geologists (scientists who study rocks) use to identify minerals. Direct students to read the passage and complete the activities.

Day Three

Vocabulary: *cleavage, fracture*

Materials: page 101; examples or pictures of stone tools (optional)

When introducing the vocabulary, explain that geologists doing fieldwork often carry rock hammers so that they can break open rocks; doing this reveals two more characteristics of minerals—*cleavage* and *fracture.* After students have read the passage and completed the activities, review the answers together. For activity B, you may wish to bring in examples or pictures of a stone ax head or arrowhead.

Day Four

Vocabulary: *hardness*

Materials: page 102; baby powder with talc (optional)

Introduce the vocabulary word and point out the Mohs hardness scale on the page. Explain that hardness or softness of a mineral can be very useful. If you have it, pass around the baby powder and tell students that talc is used in baby powder because it is such a soft mineral that it won't irritate the skin. After students have read the passage, confirm students' understanding that a mineral cannot be scratched by a mineral that is softer than itself. Have them complete the activities.

Day Five

Materials: page 103

Have students complete the page independently. Then review the answers together.

Name _____

Weekly Question

Day 1 What's the difference between a rock and a mineral?

A **mineral** is a nonliving solid that occurs in nature and has a **crystalline** structure. This means that the atoms in the mineral are arranged in a certain order and are regularly spaced apart. Salt is a mineral with a crystalline structure. If you look closely, each grain of salt is shaped more or less like a cube. This is why some people refer to salt as "salt crystals."

Different atoms combine to make different minerals. Many minerals are formed deep in Earth's crust where there is a lot of heat and pressure. As liquid magma from Earth's mantle cools into solid rock, minerals form within the rock. So, all rocks are actually made up of different minerals.

Different amounts of heat and pressure form different minerals. But not all minerals form from cooling magma. Some, like salt, are formed when water evaporates and leaves minerals behind.

Vocabulary

crystalline
KRISS-tal-lin
having a repeating, ordered, inside structure

minerals
MIN-er-ulz
naturally-occurring, non-living solids that have a crystalline structure

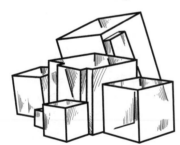

magnified salt crystals

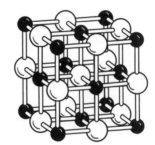

atoms in a salt crystal

A. What are the two ways that minerals can form?

1. _____   2. _____

B. Write *true* or *false*.

1. Crystals have random structures.   _____

2. Minerals occur in nature.   _____

3. All rocks contain minerals.   _____

Name _____

Day 2

Weekly Question

What's the difference between a rock and a mineral?

Daily Science

Big Idea 4

WEEK 1

Minerals are commonly identified by their physical properties. Two properties used to identify minerals are **color** and **streak**. *Streak* describes the mark left behind after rubbing a mineral on a hard, rough, white surface. Surprisingly, the color of a mineral and the color of its streak can be different. For example, the mineral pyrite (PIE-rite), or "fool's gold," has a color very similar to gold. Real gold has a yellowish streak. But pyrite, which contains only iron and sulfur, has a greenish black streak.

Minerals can also be identified by their **luster**, or shininess. A mineral's luster might be glassy, waxy, pearly, metallic, or earthy. Quartz has a glassy luster, while silver is metallic.

streak

Vocabulary

color
KUH-ler
the color or range of colors that a mineral usually appears to be

luster
LUSS-tur
the way in which the surface of a mineral reflects light

streak
streek
the mark left behind after rubbing a mineral on a hard, rough, white surface

A. Use the vocabulary words to complete the sentences.

1. People who like shiny minerals would pay attention to

    a mineral's _____.

2. If you want to draw a four-square grid on the blacktop,

    you would want a mineral with a white _____.

3. Diamonds may be clear or have a yellow, blue, or pink _____.

B. Why do you suppose geologists (scientists who study rocks) use more than one property to identify minerals?

_____

_____

Name _____

Day 3

Weekly Question

What's the difference between a rock and a mineral?

Some minerals look very similar—until they break! For example, both hematite (HEE-muh-tite) and mica (MIKE-uh) are minerals that can be black or silvery gray. So how can you tell them apart?

Hit mica with a hammer, and it splits into flat sheets. Hit hematite, and it shatters into jagged pieces. The property of breaking along regular, smooth surfaces is called **cleavage**. Mica has nearly perfect cleavage, while hematite doesn't have cleavage. Instead, hematite has a property called **fracture**, which means that it breaks along irregular, jagged surfaces. Geologists use fracture and cleavage to study rocks in places where the only equipment they may have is their eyes and a hammer.

Vocabulary

cleavage
CLEE-vej
the way some minerals break along flat planes to form regular shapes

fracture
FRAK-chur
the way minerals can break into random pieces with no regular shape

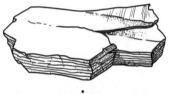

mica

hematite

A. Write whether each mineral described shows *cleavage* or *fracture*.

1. When opal breaks, it creates many uneven pieces. _____

2. When calcite breaks, it creates flat, shiny surfaces. _____

3. When jadeite breaks, it forms sharp splinters. _____

4. When augite breaks, it forms nearly perfect prisms. _____

B. Early hunters made axes and arrowheads from rocks. Do you think they chose rocks that had *cleavage* or *fracture*? Why?

_____

_____

Name _____

Daily Science

Big Idea 4

WEEK 1

A diamond is often described as the hardest mineral on Earth. **Hardness** is a property of minerals that describes how easily a mineral can be scratched. Mineral hardness is ranked from 1 to 10 on the Mohs (moaz) hardness scale, with 10 being the hardest. Diamonds are a 10 on the Mohs scale! Only a diamond can scratch another diamond. Minerals such as talc and mica, on the other hand, are so soft that you can scratch them with your fingernail.

Vocabulary

hardness
HARD-niss
describes how easily a mineral can be scratched

A. Use the chart to complete the sentences below.

Hardness scale	Material	Can be scratched by	Hardness scale	Material	Can be scratched by
1	Talc	fingernail	6	Orthoclase	pocketknife
2	Gypsum	fingernail	7	Quartz	steel file
3	Calcite	penny	8	Topaz	sandpaper
4	Fluorite	iron nail	9	Corundum	knife sharpener
5	Apatite	glass	10	Diamond	diamond

1. If a mineral can be scratched by a penny, its hardness is no greater than _____.

2. A mineral that can't be scratched by a pocketknife but can be scratched by a steel file is _____.

3. A mineral that can be scratched by glass but can't be scratched by fluorite must have a hardness between _____.

B. Drills used for making tunnels or deep holes often have diamonds in their tips. Why do you think this is?

_____

Name _____

Day 5

Weekly Question

What's the difference between a rock and a mineral?

A. Use the words in the box to complete the sentences.

> luster   fracture   cleavage   crystalline
> streak   minerals   hardness   color

1. Rocks are made of many _____.

2. A mineral showing the property of _____ breaks unevenly.

3. If a mineral shows _____, it breaks along flat planes.

4. Fool's gold has the same _____ as gold, but its

   _____ is different.

5. The property of _____ determines how easily a mineral can be scratched.

6. Pyrite, silver, and copper have a metallic _____.

7. A _____ structure has atoms that are regularly spaced.

B. Write the name of a mineral property that each tool is used to identify.

> cleavage   color   fracture   luster   streak

1. rock hammer   _____ or _____

2. white tile   _____

3. your eyes only   _____ or _____

Daily Science

Big Idea 4

The properties of rocks and minerals reflect the process that formed them.

Week 2
Where do rocks come from?

Rocks on Earth are continuously created, destroyed, and altered by processes of weathering and erosion, as well as processes of rock formation happening beneath Earth's crust. This week, students learn that over time, the cycling and transformation of rocks creates new rocks with different properties.

Rocks can be divided into three main types: igneous, sedimentary, and metamorphic. The appearance and characteristics of each rock type reflect the processes that form them. Rocks within a rock type also differ—for example, pumice and granite are both igneous rocks with different properties. If rock samples are available, it is helpful to have them for students to inspect throughout the week.

Day One

Vocabulary: *igneous*

Materials: page 105; samples of pumice, basalt, and granite (optional)

Explain that this week, students will learn about the three types of rock and how each type is formed. Introduce the vocabulary word and distribute rock samples if you have them. After students read the passage, direct them to complete the activity. When they have finished, invite volunteers to read the sentences aloud.

Day Two

Vocabulary: *cement, sediment, sedimentary*

Materials: page 106; sedimentary rocks such as sandstone, shale, and limestone (optional)

Distribute samples of sedimentary rocks if you have them. Ask students for words that describe the samples. (e.g., layered, striped) Introduce the vocabulary and direct students to read the passage. Then call students' attention to the pictures in the activity. Have students study the pictures and then determine which paragraph of the passage is being illustrated. Then direct students to complete the activity. Review students' responses before conducting the oral activity.

Day Three

Vocabulary: *metamorphic*

Materials: page 107; samples of metamorphic rocks such as marble or slate (optional)

Distribute rock samples if you have them. Tell students they will learn how these rocks are different from igneous and sedimentary rocks. After you introduce the vocabulary word, ask students to visualize the process being described as they read the passage. Then have students complete the activities. Review the answers together.

Day Four

Vocabulary: *rock cycle*

Materials: page 108

Remind students that on Day 3 they learned how heat and pressure can change igneous and sedimentary rocks into metamorphic rocks. Tell them that today they will learn how rocks are always changing from one form into another. After students have read the passage, take time to examine and discuss the rock cycle diagram.

Day Five

Materials: page 109

Have students complete the page independently. Then review the answers together.

Name _____

Day 1

Weekly Question

Where do rocks come from?

Scientists divide rocks into three types according to how the rocks are formed. Rock that forms when hot, liquid rock cools and hardens is called **igneous** rock. The properties of an igneous rock are determined by how fast the molten rock cools.

When igneous rock cools slowly under the ground, the minerals in the rock have time to form large, visible crystals. Granite is an example of this kind of igneous rock. In contrast, basalt (buh-SALT) and pumice (PUH-miss) are igneous rocks that form from lava flowing from a volcano. Mineral crystals in these rocks are often too small to see without a strong microscope. These rocks cool above ground and harden quickly. Pumice is very light and airy, while basalt is much denser.

Vocabulary

igneous
IG-nee-us
a type of rock that forms when molten rock cools

basalt   pumice   granite

Use information from the passage to complete the sentences.

1. When lava cools, it forms _____ rock.

2. The size of igneous rock _____ depends on how quickly the rock cools.

3. An igneous rock that is so light it can float on water is _____.

4. An igneous rock that forms large crystals is _____.

5. Without a _____, it can be difficult to see the crystals in basalt.

Name _____

Day 2

Weekly Question

Where do rocks come from?

Sedimentary rock is a kind of rock created from **sediment**, which can come from several sources. For instance, the weathering and erosion of larger rocks can create sediment made of smaller rocks and sand. Over time, heat and pressure can cause sediment to **cement** together and form solid rock. Shale is a sedimentary rock formed from mud.

Other kinds of sediment are created in the ocean from the shells of tiny organisms that settle on the seafloor. As layers of sediment pile up, the weight of the sediment squeezes water out of the spaces between the shells. Heat, pressure, and time work to cement the bits of shell into rock. Limestone is a sedimentary rock formed this way.

In the circles, number the pictures to show the order in which sedimentary rock can be formed. In each box, write the letter of the caption that goes with the picture.

a. **Buried sediment, affected by heat and pressure, forms rock.**

b. **Sedimentary rock can be exposed by uplift caused by earthquakes.**

c. **Sediment from microscopic shells builds up on the seafloor.**

Vocabulary

cement
suh-MENT
to glue together and become solid

sediment
SED-uh-ment
a naturally-occurring deposit of small rocks, sand, or the remains of plants and animals

sedimentary
SED-uh-MEN-tuh-ree
formed from sediment

Talk

How is it possible that limestone deposits containing a lot of shells can be found many miles from a body of water?

Name _____

Day 3

Weekly Question

Where do rocks come from?

Great heat and pressure, such as the kind that occurs deep within Earth, can cause rocks to change. Rock that changes this way is called **metamorphic** rock. With enough heat, pressure, and time, both igneous and sedimentary rocks can be transformed into metamorphic rocks.

Metamorphic rocks tend to be harder than other kinds of rocks. They are often striped or show a swirled pattern. Where does this pattern come from? When a rock is heated, different-colored parts of the rock can start to melt, like chocolate chips do when cookies are baked. If the rock is then squeezed by pressure, the soft, melted parts can flow. This is what gives the rock stripes or swirls. Marble, which is formed from limestone, is a kind of metamorphic rock. Slate, which is formed from shale, is another kind.

Vocabulary

metamorphic
MET-uh-MOR-fik
a type of rock that has been physically changed by heat or pressure

A. This diagram shows how metamorphic rock forms. Draw arrows and label them to show where the *heat* and *pressure* come from.

Earth's surface

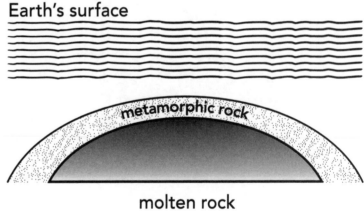

molten rock

B. Use information from the passage to complete the sentences.

1. _____ and _____ can transform one kind of rock into another over a long period of time.

2. Marble is an example of _____ rock.

3. Stripes in metamorphic rock form when parts of the rock

   _____.

Name _____

Day 4

Weekly Question

Where do rocks come from?

Big Idea 4

Daily Science

WEEK 2

Rocks are constantly changed by processes on and within Earth. Weathering and erosion break down rocks into sediment. Heat and pressure in Earth's crust change rocks into new kinds. In addition, the movement of Earth's plates allows rocks in the crust to sink back into the mantle and melt. Magma from the mantle can then rise through cracks in the crust and form new rocks. This natural process of creation, destruction, and recycling of rock material between the mantle and Earth's surface is called the **rock cycle**.

Vocabulary

rock cycle
rock SY-kul
natural process of creation, destruction, and recycling of rocks in Earth's crust and upper mantle

Use the diagram of the rock cycle to complete the sentences below.

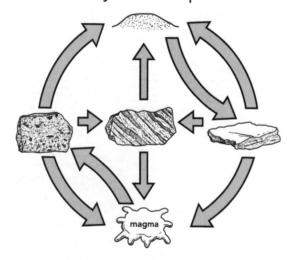

magma

1. Heat and pressure turn igneous rock or sedimentary rock

   into _____ rock.

2. Magma cools to become _____.

3. Weathering and erosion turn rock into _____.

4. Cementing results in _____ rock.

5. When rocks melt, they become _____.

Name _____

Day 5

Weekly Question

Where do rocks come from?

A. Use the words in the box to complete the sentences.

> igneous   cement   sedimentary
> sediment   rock cycle   metamorphic

1. When lava or magma cools, it forms _____ rocks.

2. All rocks are created, changed, or destroyed in the _____.

3. _____ rocks are formed when other rocks are weathered

   or eroded and leave behind _____.

4. Pressure causes sediment to _____ and form a hard rock.

5. A _____ rock forms when another rock is subjected to

   a lot of heat and pressure.

B. Name one trait of each type of rock and describe how the rock is formed.

1. Igneous: _____

2. Metamorphic: _____

3. Sedimentary: _____

C. Add the missing words to complete three parts of the rock cycle.

1. Igneous rock + _____ and _____ = sedimentary rock

2. Sedimentary rock + _____ and _____ = metamorphic rock

3. Magma + _____ = igneous rock

The properties of rocks and minerals reflect the process that formed them.

Week 3
Are some rocks valuable?

Students may have a general sense of what a natural resource is (air, water, trees), but they may have difficulty identifying natural resources that are dug out of the ground. Natural resources that contain minerals—such as gold and iron—as well as fossil fuels, are nonrenewable. This makes them valuable for both their usefulness and limited availability. Some nonrenewable resources are available but not easily obtainable without further improvements in technology or a substantial impact on the environment, such as with offshore drilling for oil. This week, students will learn about some of these resources, including how they are created, extracted, and used.

Day One

Vocabulary: *natural resources*

Materials: page 111

Activate prior knowledge by asking students to list as many natural resources as they can think of. (e.g., water, trees, oil, sunlight, wind) Introduce the vocabulary word to clarify students' thinking about what a natural resource is. After students have finished reading the passage, guide them through the illustration and have them complete the activity. Review the answers together.

Day Two

Vocabulary: *carbon, fossil fuels*

Materials: page 112; charcoal (optional)

Introduce the vocabulary. If you have it, show students the charcoal and explain that charcoal is mostly carbon and, like other fossil fuels, it can be used as a source of energy. After students finish reading, direct them to complete the activities. Review the answers together. If you wish to extend the lesson, consider explaining to students how fossil fuels are often used in ways other than to produce energy. For example, oil is used to make plastic.

Day Three

Vocabulary: *extract, metals, ore*

Materials: page 113

Point out all the things made of metal in the classroom and ask students to imagine how different life would be without this natural resource. Introduce the vocabulary and point out the illustration on the page. After students have finished reading, direct them to complete activities A and B independently. For the oral activity, pair students or discuss as a group. You may wish to build background by explaining more about the gold rush from the mid-1800s prior to completing the activity.

Day Four

Vocabulary: *conserve, renewable*

Materials: page 114

Introduce the vocabulary. When students have finished reading, confirm students' understanding that fossil fuels and metals are nonrenewable. Then have students complete the activities independently. Review the answers together.

Day Five

Materials: page 115

Have students complete the page independently. Then review the answers together.

Name _____

Day 1

Weekly Question

Are some rocks valuable?

If you were to name some **natural resources**, you might include the air, water, plants, and animals that exist all around us. Natural resources also include materials we dig out of the ground. Iron and limestone are natural resources, and so are coal, oil, and natural gas.

These underground resources are found in rocks or in pockets between rock layers. These materials have many uses. We use natural resources to make the steel and cement necessary to build cities and to create the energy that we use to power our growing, modern world.

Vocabulary

natural resources
NACH-er-ul
REE-sor-sez
useful materials or sources of energy found on Earth

Fill in the chart with the natural resources listed in the passage.

Natural resources found above ground	Natural resources dug out of the ground

Name _____

Day 2

Weekly Question

Are some rocks valuable?

Coal, oil, and natural gas are a group of natural resources called **fossil fuels**. For many years, they have been the source of the energy we use to heat our homes and run our cars and other machines.

Fossil fuels get their name from the way they were created. Hundreds of millions of years ago, the decaying remains of plants and animals built up at the bottom of swamps and shallow seas. These remains were rich in **carbon**. Eventually, the mud and sediment surrounding the material became sedimentary rock. Heat, time, and pressure caused some of the carbon-rich remains to turn into coal, pools of oil, or pockets of natural gas.

Although the processes that create fossil fuels are still at work, it would take millions of years to replace the oil, coal, and natural gas that we have already used.

Vocabulary

carbon
KAR-bun
an element found in all living things

fossil fuels
FOS-sil fyoolz
fuels formed from the fossilized remains of plants and animals

A. Number the pictures in order to show how fossil fuels are created and removed from the ground.

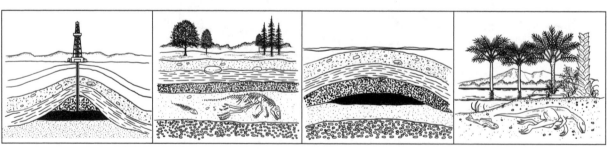

___   ___   ___   ___

B. Write *true* or *false*.

1. Fossil fuels come from the carbon-rich remains of organisms that lived hundreds of millions of years ago.   _____

2. Fossil fuels can be replaced as quickly as they are used.   _____

Name _____

Day 3

Weekly Question

Are some rocks valuable?

Metals are another natural resource found in the ground. They are used for many things, from gold jewelry to the steel beams in large buildings. Metals are found in rocks. Metal-rich rocks and sediment are called **ores**.

Ores can be removed from the ground by mining the surrounding rock. When the ore lies close to Earth's surface, it can often be dug out of the ground or removed with water. In many cases, however, valuable ores lie deep in the ground. Powerful drills are used to tunnel into the rock, and special machines **extract** the ore.

A. Use the vocabulary words to label the illustration and complete the sentence.

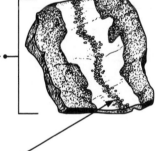

People often use machines to _____ natural resources from the ground.

B. Complete the analogy.

Metal is to *ore* as _____.

☐ rock is to *natural resource*   ☐ mineral is to *rock*

☐ fossil fuel is to *energy*   ☐ natural resource is to *tree*

Vocabulary

extract
ek-STRAKT
to remove

metals
MET-ulz
minerals that are usually hard and shiny, conduct electricity and heat, and can be melted and formed into shapes

ore
or
rock or sediment that contains metal

Talk

In the 1800s, people went to California to get rich looking for gold. Do you think these people mined ore close to the surface or deep in the ground? What methods do you think they used? Discuss it with a partner.

Name _____

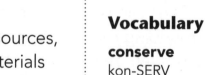

Daily Science

Big Idea 4

WEEK 3

Earth's supply of fossil fuels, metals, and other minerals is limited. Materials dug out of the ground are not **renewable** in the way that lumber from a forest is. Forests can be regrown by planting new trees, but scientists cannot make more iron and gold in the laboratory.

Because Earth has limited mineral and fossil fuel resources, scientists are seeking to invent strong, new building materials from substances that are plentiful, such as ground-up rock. They are also trying to find better ways to use plentiful energy sources, such as solar and wind power. In addition, there is now greater interest in, as well as reasons for, finding ways to **conserve** and reuse Earth's valuable materials.

Vocabulary

conserve
kon-SERV
to save or use sparingly

renewable
ree-NEW-ah-bul
able to be replaced by a new supply

A. Write *true* or *false*.

1. Earth has unlimited natural resources. _____

2. Forests are renewable resources. _____

3. Scientists can make gold in the laboratory. _____

4. Solar and wind energy sources won't run out. _____

5. Minerals are renewable. _____

B. Many people involved in conserving resources use the slogan "reduce, reuse, recycle." How would doing each of these things help conserve natural resources? Explain why.

_____

_____

_____

Name _____

Day 5

Weekly Question

Are some rocks valuable?

A. Use the words in the box to complete the sentences.

> ore   metals   conserve   renewable
>
> carbon   extract   fossil fuel   natural resource

1. Trees are a _____ that is _____.

2. Coal is a _____ made from organisms that

    contain the element _____.

3. _____ is rock that contains _____.

4. People _____ resources to keep from running out.

5. Machines _____ ore from deep within the ground.

B. Fill in the chart to describe the role that fossil fuels and metals
play in your life.

Fossil fuels I use:	How I use them:
1. _____	1. _____
2. _____	2. _____

Metals I use:	How I use them:
1. _____	1. _____
2. _____	2. _____

Daily Science

Big Idea 4

The properties of rocks and minerals reflect the process that formed them.

Week 4
Do all rocks come from Earth?

Although the vast majority of rock on Earth originated on this planet, some of the rocks and minerals came from space. Most of these samples came from asteroids in our solar system, though we have found rocks from both the Moon and Mars. Scientists looking to learn more about the Moon and Mars have sent astronauts and robots to study the rocks and minerals and sometimes return with samples. These studies and samples have helped scientists learn more about the origin of planets and moons in our solar system. Similarities in lunar and Earth rocks have convinced many scientists that the Moon was once part of Earth. They feel that the Moon was formed after a large impact broke away part of Earth very early in the planet's history. This week, students learn about extraterrestrial rocks and their similarities to and differences from rocks and minerals on Earth.

Day One

Vocabulary: *meteor, meteorite*

Materials: page 117

Ask students if they have ever seen a "shooting star" and invite volunteers to describe what it looked like. Introduce the vocabulary, making sure to explain that a meteor is the glowing trail and not the falling object. Point out the picture on the page and explain that the meteorite was found in Willamette, Oregon, but is now on display in New York. When students have finished reading the passage, have them complete the activities. Review the answers together.

Day Two

Vocabulary: *asteroids*

Materials: page 118

Introduce the vocabulary word and point out the asteroid belt on the page. After students have finished reading, direct them to complete the activities independently. Review the answers together.

Day Three

Vocabulary: *lunar, maria*

Materials: page 119

Have students discuss what they think the surface of the Moon is like and what similarities and differences there might be between Earth rocks and lunar rocks. Then introduce the vocabulary. Point out that *maria* is the Latin word for "seas." The name comes from early scientists who mistook these patches for bodies of water. When students have finished reading, have them complete the activities. Review the answers together.

Day Four

Vocabulary: *extraterrestrial*

Materials: page 120

Introduce the vocabulary word and explain that anything coming from space is considered to be "extraterrestrial." After students have finished reading, explain that scientists are looking for both fossil evidence and evidence of water on Mars, as water is necessary for life as we know it. Have students complete the activities. Review the answers together.

Day Five

Materials: page 121

Have students complete the page independently. Then review the answers together.

Name _____

Day 1

Weekly Question

Do all rocks come from Earth?

You might call them "shooting stars," but scientists call the streaks of light you sometimes see flash across the night sky **meteors**. Meteors are bright streaks that are created when rocks or other solid objects from outer space heat up and glow as they fall through Earth's atmosphere. Usually, the objects burn up quickly in the atmosphere and never hit the ground. But if a space rock does land on Earth's surface, it is called a **meteorite**.

Meteorites can look and feel different from other rocks. They can be very heavy, have an unusual shape, and show signs of having melted. If you find a rock like this and it is very different from other rocks in the area, it could be a meteorite.

The Willamette meteorite is the largest meteorite ever discovered in the United States. It weighs over 15 tons.

Vocabulary

meteor
MEE-tee-yor
the glowing trail created by a solid object as it falls through Earth's atmosphere and heats up

meteorite
MEE-tee-yor-ITE
an object from space that hits Earth's surface

A. What four characteristics would help you determine if a rock could be a meteorite?

1. _____ 3. _____

2. _____ 4. _____

B. According to the passage, what is the difference between a meteor and a meteorite?

_____

_____

Name _____

Day 2

Weekly Question

Do all rocks come from Earth?

Most meteorites come from a part of the solar system that is home to many small, rocky bodies called **asteroids**. Asteroids are much smaller than planets, and most of the ones in our solar system exist between Mars and Jupiter. Because asteroids are so small and so far away, scientists have many questions about them, including exactly what they are made of.

Although much about asteroids is unknown, meteorites that come from asteroids give scientists more clues. Iron meteorites, which are almost pure metal, may be the cores of asteroids. Stony meteorites, on the other hand, have minerals that are similar to minerals in Earth's crust and mantle. In the future, we may be able to extract these natural resources from asteroids and use them back on Earth.

Vocabulary

asteroids
AS-ter-oydz
small bodies of solid rock that orbit the sun

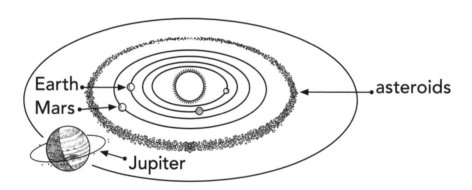

A. Why do scientists have difficulty studying asteroids?

_____

B. Write *true* or *false.*

   1. Some meteorites contain iron.   _____

   2. Some asteroids contain part of Earth's crust.   _____

   3. Asteroids are smaller than planets.   _____

Name _____

Weekly Question

Do all rocks come from Earth?

Meteorites are only one example of the rocks that exist in our solar system. In the late 1960s and early 1970s, astronauts went to the Moon and brought back 842 pounds of **lunar** rocks. There are differences and similarities between lunar and Earth rocks. One difference is that there are fewer minerals in lunar rocks than in Earth rocks. Also, lunar rocks are not changed by weathering or erosion the way that Earth rocks are. This is because the Moon has no atmosphere or flowing water.

Lunar and Earth rocks also have some similarities. For example, lunar dust contains high amounts of calcium, iron, and aluminum, which are all commonly found in rocks on Earth. Also, scientists have determined that lava once flowed across the Moon's surface, forming rock in the same way that it does on Earth. These lava flows created large, dark patches on the Moon, which we call **maria**.

Vocabulary

lunar
LOO-nar
related to or coming from the Moon

maria
MAR-ee-ah
plains of dark basalt rock visible on the Moon's surface

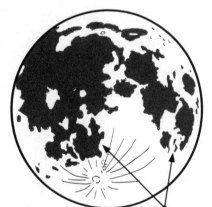

maria

A. What kind of rock makes up the Moon's maria—*sedimentary*, *igneous*, or *metamorphic*? Explain how you know.

_____

_____

B. Name two ways lunar rocks are similar to Earth rocks and two ways they are different.

Similar: **1.** _____   **2.** _____

Different: **1.** _____   **2.** _____

Name _____

Day 4

Weekly Question

Do all rocks come from Earth?

Of all the rocky places in outer space, Mars is the most like Earth. Mars has volcanoes, canyons, and rocks very similar to those on Earth. Mars gets its red color from rocks containing the iron-rich mineral hematite, which is very common on Earth. But Mars also has unusual minerals that are not found on Earth.

So far, scientists have found 34 meteorites from Mars. These rocks contain some of the special minerals that exist only on Mars, and some even show evidence of what might be bacteria fossils. This has prompted scientists to send robots to Mars to study the planet directly. They are hoping to find more proof of **extraterrestrial** life, as well as to learn more about how Mars and Earth were formed.

Vocabulary

extraterrestrial
EK-struh-tuh-RES-tree-ul
not from Earth

A. Underline the information in the passage that proves Mars has experienced weathering and erosion.

B. What kind of Mars rock might contain fossils: *sedimentary*, *igneous*, or *metamorphic*? Explain how you know.

_____

_____

_____

Name _____

Day 5

Weekly Question

Do all rocks come from Earth?

A. Use the words in the box to complete the paragraph.

> asteroid   lunar   extraterrestrial
>
> meteor   maria   meteorite

The glowing streak of light from a rock in Earth's atmosphere is a

_____, but if the rock strikes Earth's surface, it becomes

a _____. If the rock came from the Moon, we would

call it a _____ rock, and it could have come from the

dark spots on the Moon's surface called _____. If the

rock came from Mars, it could contain proof of _____

life. Most likely, though, the rock came from an _____

floating between Mars and Jupiter.

B. Complete the chart to show how each type of rock is similar to
and different from Earth rocks.

	Like Earth rocks	Different from Earth rocks
Lunar rocks	1. _____ 2. _____	1. _____ 2. _____
Mars rocks	1. _____ 2. _____	1. _____

Name _____

Unit Review

Comprehension

Rocks and Minerals

A. Fill in the bubble next to the correct answer.

1. What type of rock would likely contain a fossil fuel?

   Ⓐ metamorphic   Ⓒ sedimentary

   Ⓑ igneous   Ⓓ mineral

2. Along with heat and time, what else does a metamorphic rock need in order to form?

   Ⓐ water   Ⓒ sediment

   Ⓑ pressure   Ⓓ lava

3. Which of these is NOT a property of metal?

   Ⓐ found in ore   Ⓒ is renewable

   Ⓑ is a mineral   Ⓓ is hard and shiny

4. Which of these is NOT a property used to identify a mineral?

   Ⓐ color   Ⓒ cleavage

   Ⓑ streak   Ⓓ weight

5. What type of rock makes up the dark spots on the Moon?

   Ⓐ igneous   Ⓒ sedimentary

   Ⓑ metamorphic   Ⓓ mineral

B. List two properties used to identify minerals and explain what each property describes.

   1. _____

   2. _____

Unit Review

Vocabulary

Rock-Solid Vocabulary

Next to each vocabulary word, write the letter of its definition.

_____ **1.** asteroids

_____ **2.** cleavage

_____ **3.** conserve

_____ **4.** crystalline

_____ **5.** extract

_____ **6.** fracture

_____ **7.** hardness

_____ **8.** igneous

_____ **9.** lunar

_____ **10.** luster

_____ **11.** metals

_____ **12.** metamorphic

_____ **13.** meteorite

_____ **14.** minerals

_____ **15.** natural resources

_____ **16.** ore

_____ **17.** renewable

_____ **18.** rock cycle

_____ **19.** sediment

_____ **20.** sedimentary

a. to save

b. all rocks are made of these

c. an object from space that strikes Earth

d. the property that describes how easy it is to scratch a mineral

e. things that come from the Moon

f. rock formed from cooled lava

g. able to be replaced by a new supply

h. rock that has changed because of intense heat and pressure

i. useful materials or resources from nature

j. having a repeated, ordered structure

k. to remove

l. gold and iron are examples

m. the way a mineral breaks along flat, even planes

n. small deposits of rock, sand, or plant and animal remains

o. the shininess of a mineral

p. rock or sediment that contains metal

q. the way a mineral breaks into jagged, irregular pieces

r. limestone and sandstone are examples

s. how rock is constantly created, changed, and broken down

t. small bodies of rock between Mars and Jupiter

Name _____

Mineral Mysteries

This chart lists several properties of different minerals.
Use it to answer the questions below.

Name	Color	Hardness	Streak	Luster	Cleavage or Fracture
graphite	silver or black	1–1.5	black	metallic	perfect cleavage
calcite	white or colorless	3	white	glassy	perfect cleavage
apatite	green	5	white	glassy	fracture
hematite	steel gray	5–6	red	metallic	fracture
quartz	white or colorless	7	white	glassy	poor cleavage

1. Which is the softest mineral that can be colorless? _____

2. Which mineral can be white and has poor cleavage? _____

3. Which is the softest mineral with a metallic luster? _____

4. Three minerals have a white streak. Which mineral can scratch the other minerals? _____

5. Two minerals of similar hardness do not have cleavage. Which has a glassy luster? _____

6. Which mineral's color is different from its streak and also has a metallic luster? _____

Name _____

Unit Review

Hands-on Activity
Chalk It Up to Science

The expression "hard as a rock" suggests that rocks are always hard. But some rocks are harder than others, and some will fall apart more easily than others. In this experiment, you will see what happens to chalk, which is a form of limestone.

What You Need

- two small glass or plastic containers
- 1/2 cup water
- 1/2 cup vinegar
- box of chalk
- rubber gloves

1. Put on the rubber gloves and assemble all the materials on a table.

2. Pour the vinegar into one of the containers and water into the other.

3. Break a piece of chalk into four pieces and drop two pieces into each container. Make sure the chalk is the same size for each container.

What Did You Discover?

1. Compare the chalk in the water to the chalk in the vinegar. Which changed more? What happened?

_____

2. Why do you think it helps to break the chalk into many pieces?

_____

3. Limestone is found in many water supplies and can build up on kitchen and bathroom surfaces. If you were developing a cleaning product, why might you want to include vinegar as an ingredient?

_____

Big Idea 5

Electrical energy can be converted into heat, light, sound, and motion.

Key Concept
Electrical energy can be converted into other forms of energy.

National Standard
Electricity in circuits can produce light, heat, sound, and magnetic effects.

By fourth grade, students have a basic understanding that electricity is a form of energy that powers lights, appliances, and toys. However, students are probably not aware of the processes that allow electricity to change into other forms of energy. This Big Idea teaches students the following:

→ how electricity is converted into heat;

→ how electricity is converted into light;

→ how electricity is converted into sound; and

→ how electricity is converted into mechanical energy.

Teacher Background

There's no doubt that electricity plays a very important role in the lives of modern human beings. Electrical energy provides power to devices old and new—from toasters and hearing aids to LED lights and electric cars. But electricity not only powers these machines, it also provides heat, light, sound, and movement. This unit deals with the idea that electrical energy can be converted into other forms.

Electric current flowing through a circuit is a form of energy. When electrical energy flows in a circuit connected to a resistor, it can change into heat. When an electric current passes through an electric motor, it changes into mechanical energy. The microphone and the speaker of a hearing aid convert sound waves into electricity and back again. And electric current that flows through an LED turns into light.

For specific background information on each week's concepts, refer to the notes on pp. 128, 134, 140, and 146.

WEEK 1: How do toasters work?

Connection to the Big Idea: Filaments in toasters convert electrical energy into heat. This week, students learn how electric current flows through a circuit. They discover how a resistor is different from a conductor and learn the role it plays in converting electrical energy into heat.

Content Vocabulary: *circuit, conductor, electric current, filaments, radiate, resistor, switch*

WEEK 2: What lights a digital clock?

Connection to the Big Idea: The LEDs (light-emitting diodes) in a digital clock convert electrical energy into light. This week, students learn what an LED is and discover how electric current flows through a digital clock. They then learn that when the current reaches the LED, electrons release energy in the form of light.

Content Vocabulary: *display, electron, LED, photon*

WEEK 3: How do hearing aids help people hear?

Connection to the Big Idea: Hearing aids convert sound waves into an electronic signal and then change the signal back into sound waves. This week, students learn that sound waves travel as waves of energy. They learn about the parts of a hearing aid and discover how each part helps turn the sound energy into electrical energy and then back into sound energy.

Content Vocabulary: *amplifier, electromagnet, hearing aid, microphone, sound waves, speaker*

WEEK 4: How do electric cars work?

Connection to the Big Idea: Electric cars work by using electric motors that convert electrical energy into motion. Motion is a form of mechanical energy. Students learn that an electric motor converts electrical energy into mechanical energy through the use of a permanent magnet and an electromagnet. Students then discover how components of the electric car control the amount of electrical energy a motor receives. Finally, students explore other devices that use electric motors.

Content Vocabulary: *controller, electric motor, electromagnet, magnetic force, mechanical energy*

WEEK 5: Unit Review

These activities review the key concepts of how electrical energy is converted into other forms of energy.

p. 152: Comprehension Students answer multiple-choice items that review key concepts from the unit.

p. 153: Vocabulary Students match key vocabulary words from the unit with their definitions.

p. 154: Visual Literacy Students study different electronic devices and determine the types of energy these devices convert electrical energy into.

p. 155: Hands-on Activity Students create an electric "motor." Review the materials and instructions on the student page ahead of time.

Daily Science

Big Idea 5

Electrical energy can be converted into heat, light, sound, and motion.

Week 1
How do toasters work?

This week, students learn that a toaster is an example of how electrical energy is converted into heat. A toaster is a simple appliance that sends electric current through a circuit, which is completed or broken by the switch that raises and lowers the toast. Part of the circuit consists of exposed filaments that act as resistors. The resistors limit the amount of electric current flowing through the circuit and convert some of the electrical energy into heat energy. When hot, the filaments radiate heat energy that toasts the bread.

Day One

Vocabulary: *circuit, electric current, switch*

Materials: page 129

Since the purpose of this week is to explain how electric energy can be converted into heat energy, the basics of electricity, electric current, and circuits will not be discussed in depth. You may wish to review these concepts with students as you introduce the vocabulary. You may also wish to complete the activities as a group to make sure students understand what a circuit is and how electric current flows through it.

Day Two

Vocabulary: *conductor, resistor*

Materials: page 130

Before students read the passage, activate prior knowledge by reminding them what conductors are and helping them think of some examples. (Conductors conduct electric current; examples include copper wire, water, steel poles, etc.) After students have finished reading, direct them to complete the activities. Review the answers together.

Day Three

Vocabulary: *filaments, radiate*

Materials: page 131; toaster (optional)

Introduce the vocabulary and, if you have a toaster, allow students to look inside it before you turn it on. Then turn it on and allow students to look from a safe distance at the toaster's filaments as they become hot. After students read the passage, direct them to complete the activities independently. Review the answers together.

Day Four

Materials: page 132

After students finish reading the passage, direct them to complete the activities. Invite volunteers to share their responses to activity B.

Day Five

Materials: page 133

Have students complete the page independently. Then review the answers together.

Daily Science • EMC 5014 • © Evan-Moor Corp.

Name _____

Day 1

Weekly Question

How do toasters work?

You probably think a toaster is a very simple appliance. After all, the only thing it does is make toast. It's true that compared to televisions and computers, toasters are pretty simple. When you push the lever down on a toaster, a **switch** completes a **circuit** that sends **electric current** flowing through the appliance. But would you guess that inventors had a very hard time inventing a toaster? In fact, it took many years to figure out a way to make a toaster that wouldn't melt or burst into flames!

A. Look at the diagram and then follow the instructions.

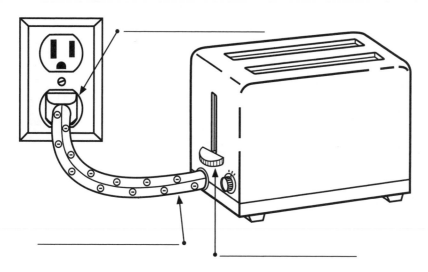

Vocabulary

circuit
SIR-kut
a loop or path along which an electric current flows

electric current
ee-LEK-trik KUR-ent
the flow of electricity

switch
swich
a part of a circuit that starts or stops the flow of electric current

1. Label these parts of the circuit: the *source* of electric power, the *switch*, and the electric *current*.

2. Draw arrows to show the path of electric current to and from the appliance.

B. Most levers on toasters automatically pop up when the toast is done. Why do you think that happens?

_____

_____

Name _____

How do toasters work?

Inventors in the early 1900s knew that electricity flowed through **conductors**, such as metal. They also knew that some metals were not as good at conducting as others. The inventors found that these metals could be used to limit the flow of electric current in a circuit. Such metals are called **resistors**.

When electric current flows through a circuit, some of that electrical energy turns into another form of energy—heat. When a resistor is added to the circuit, even more electrical energy is converted into heat. This was the result that the inventors of toasters wanted.

A. Write *true* or *false*.

1. A conductor allows electric current to flow through it easily.   _____

2. Electrical energy can make heat energy.   _____

3. Resistors convert less energy into heat than conductors do.   _____

4. All metals conduct electricity equally well.   _____

B. What is the main difference between a *conductor* and a *resistor*?

_____

C. How did resistors help the people who invented toasters? Explain your answer.

_____

Vocabulary

conductor
kun-DUK-tur
something that allows electric current to flow easily

resistor
ree-ZISS-tur
something that limits the flow of electric current through a circuit

Name _____

Day 3

Weekly Question

How do toasters work?

If you look inside a toaster as it is toasting bread, you'll notice several strips of glowing wire called **filaments**. These filaments are the resistors in the toaster's circuit. They limit the flow of electric current and convert some of the electrical energy into heat energy. That heat energy **radiates** from the filaments and toasts the bread.

When toasters were first invented, the filaments inside would get hot enough to toast bread, but they didn't last very long before they melted or burned. An inventor named Albert Marsh solved the problem. He used two metals, nickel and chromium (KRO-mee-um), to create a wire that was a good resistor and could withstand very high heat. This metal is used in toasters today.

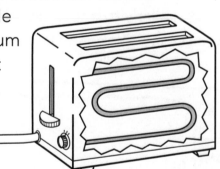

Vocabulary

filaments
FIL-uh-mentz
wires that heat up or glow when they conduct electricity

radiate
RAY-dee-ate
to send out energy in waves or rays

A. Number the events in the correct order to explain how a toaster works.

_____ The filaments radiate heat energy.

_____ Electric current completes the circuit in a toaster.

_____ Filament resistors convert some electrical energy into heat energy.

_____ The bread is toasted.

B. Most toasters allow you to set how light or dark you want your toast. What do you think changes inside the toaster, depending on the setting?

_____

C. List three other things that radiate heat energy.

1. _____   2. _____   3. _____

Name _____

Day 4

Weekly Question

How do toasters work?

Daily Science

Big Idea 5

WEEK 1

Toasters aren't the only appliances that turn electrical energy into heat energy. Electric stoves, electric blankets, irons, and even some cars convert electrical energy into heat energy. All of these inventions use filament resistors that can withstand very high temperatures. But sometimes the materials around the filaments cannot. For example, toast left in the toaster too long can turn black or even catch on fire. That's why you should never leave your toaster unattended while you're making toast.

A. A hair dryer works similarly to a toaster. Look at the diagram of the hair dryer. Where do you think the filaments are? Draw them below.

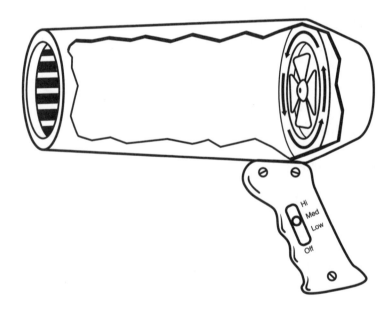

B. Today, some toasters do more than just toast bread. One toaster can "print" messages from your computer onto your toast. Another toasts pictures of cartoon characters on the bread! If you could invent a new kind of toaster, what would it do? Describe it below.

_____

_____

Name _____

Day 5

Weekly Question

How do toasters work?

A. Use the words in the box to complete the sentences.

> switch   resistor   conductor   electric current
> circuit   radiate   filaments

1. The lever on a toaster is a _____ that completes

   the _____ and allows _____

   to flow through it.

2. A _____ is good at conducting electricity, while

   a _____ limits the flow of electric current.

3. The _____ in a toaster become hot and

   _____ heat energy.

B. Look at the diagram. Label the *switch* and *filaments*. Then draw the path that the electric current travels through the toaster.

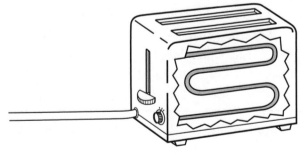

C. When people iron, they make sure to move the iron constantly around the cloth. Why is this important?

_____

_____

Daily Science

Big Idea 5

Electrical energy can be converted into heat, light, sound, and motion.

Week 2
What lights a digital clock?

This week, students learn about LEDs, or light-emitting diodes. The numbers that display the time on a digital clock are LEDs. Each digit is divided into seven segments that are separately connected to the circuit inside the clock. Each segment can turn on and off to form the correct number to tell time. When electrons in an electric current pass through an LED, the electrons get excited and emit photons of light. Compared to incandescent light bulbs, LEDs are much more energy-efficient. They may become the standard devices we use for lighting.

Day One

Vocabulary: *LED*

Materials: page 135; digital clock

Introduce the vocabulary word and show students the digital clock. Point out the LEDs on the display. Tell students that this week they will learn how an LED converts electricity into light. After students finish reading, have them complete the activities. For the oral activity, pair students or discuss the question as a group. You may want to prompt students to think about durability or brightness of LEDs, if necessary.

Day Two

Vocabulary: *display*

Materials: page 136; digital clock

Introduce the vocabulary word. Show students the digital clock. This time, ask them to look closely at the numbers to see how they are divided up into segments. After students have read the passage, have them complete the activities. Go over the answers together.

Day Three

Vocabulary: *electron, photon*

Materials: page 137

Prior to having students read the passage, you may want to review the properties of electric current and how it travels through a circuit. (Electric current is made of electrons; it travels in a loop from the power source through the circuit.) When students have finished reading, direct them to complete the activities. Review the answers together.

Day Four

Materials: page 138; compact fluorescent light, incandescent light bulb

Show students the incandescent light bulb and the compact fluorescent light. Tell students that until recently, people used mostly incandescent light bulbs in their homes. Now, a lot more people are using compact fluorescent lights (CFLs), which last longer and are more energy efficient. But even CFLs are not as efficient as LEDs. After students have read the passage, have them complete the activities. Review the answers together.

Day Five

Materials: page 139

Have students complete the page independently. Then review the answers together.

Daily Science • EMC 5014 • © Evan-Moor Corp.

Name _____

Day 1

Weekly Question

What lights a digital clock?

LEDs, or **L**ight-**E**mitting **D**iodes (DY-odz), are all around us. They form the brightly lit numbers in digital clocks. They are the tiny lights that tell us that a computer or TV is turned on. Ambulance and police siren lights often use LEDs.

Like any electrical appliance, an LED has to be connected to a source of electricity in order to work. The simplest way to describe an LED is as a tiny light bulb that fits into an electrical circuit. However, an LED is different from an ordinary light bulb because it uses less electrical energy to create an even brighter glow.

Vocabulary

LED
el-ee-dee
a device specifically made for generating light

A. Look at the diagram of a circuit. Draw an arrow pointing to the LED. Circle the electrical source.

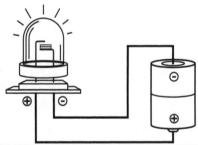

B. Write *true* or *false*.

1. Digital clocks use LEDs. _____

2. In order to work, an LED must be part of an electrical circuit. _____

3. An LED uses the same amount of energy as a light bulb to produce light. _____

 Talk

Why do you think the lights on many police cars and ambulances use LEDs? Discuss this question with a partner.

Name _____

What lights a digital clock?

When a digital clock is attached to a power source, electric current flows through the circuit to reach the LEDs in the clock's numbers. Each digit is divided into seven segments, or parts. Each segment is an LED that is connected separately to the circuit. When one of the segments receives electric current, that LED lights up. As each segment is turned on and off, the **display** on the clock changes. For example, when all seven of the LED segments in a digit are turned on, the display shows the number 8.

A device in the digital clock "counts" how long each segment receives electric current. That's how the digital clock knows when to change numbers and display the correct time.

Vocabulary

display
dih-SPLAY
information shown visually on a screen

A. Color the segments in each digit to show the time that would be displayed on this clock if:

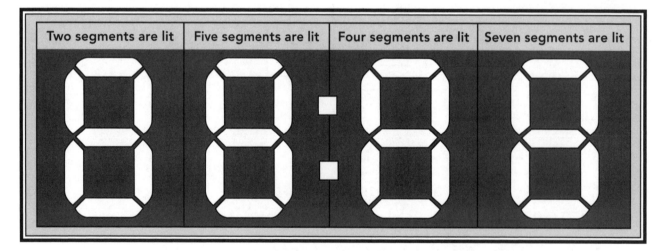

Two segments are lit	Five segments are lit	Four segments are lit	Seven segments are lit

B. If a clock reads 10:45, how many segments are lit up in all? _____

C. Name something you use that has a display. _____

Name _____

Day 3

Weekly Question

What lights a digital clock?

How exactly does an LED produce light? When electric current travels through the circuit and passes through the LED, it causes **electrons** to gain energy and become excited. These excited electrons release their extra energy in the form of light. A unit of light energy is called a **photon**. When you look at the clock to see what time it is, you are actually watching photons being released by the electrons traveling through the LED.

A. Use the vocabulary words to write a caption that explains what is happening in the illustration.

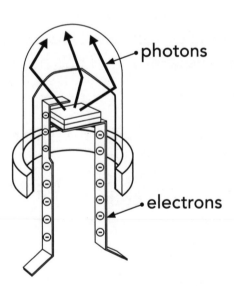

photons

electrons

Vocabulary

electron
ee-LEK-trahn
a particle of an atom with a negative charge

photon
FOE-tahn
a tiny unit of light energy

_____

B. Number the events in the correct order to explain how an LED lights up.

____ Electric current passes through the LED.

____ Excited electrons release light energy called photons.

____ The LED is connected to a power source.

____ Electrons gain energy and become excited.

____ We see the LED light up.

Name _____

Day 4

Weekly Question

What lights a digital clock?

Daily Science

Big Idea 5

WEEK 2

Today, LEDs are the most energy-efficient devices used to create light. The filament in an incandescent (IN-can-DESS-ent) light bulb wastes a lot of energy by converting most of the electricity to heat. But an LED changes most of its electrical energy into light. In addition, incandescent bulbs lose a lot of light because they shine it in all directions. This causes some of the light to be absorbed back into the bulb. LEDs shine photons in one direction, so all their light is focused and bright.

LEDs are also longer-lasting than other types of light bulbs. Incandescent light bulbs usually burn out after 900 hours. Compact fluorescent (flor-ESS-ent) lights can last up to 15,000 hours. But researchers believe LEDs can last 35,000 to 50,000 hours (or ten years)! For all of these reasons, LEDs have brightened the future of lighting.

A. Write how LEDs and incandescent bulbs are similar and different.

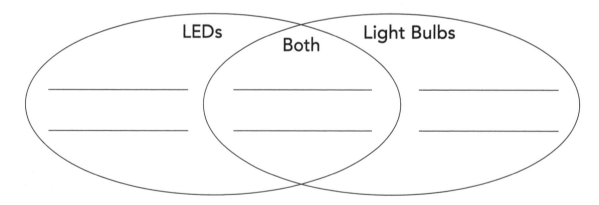

LEDs   Both   Light Bulbs

B. List three reasons why LEDs are better than incandescent light bulbs.

1. _____

2. _____

3. _____

Name _____

Day 5 *Weekly Question*

What lights a digital clock?

A. Use the words in the box to complete the paragraph.

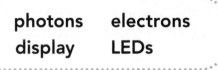

photons	electrons
display	LEDs

_____ form the brightly lit numbers of a digital clock.

Each digit on the _____ is divided into seven segments.

The segments light up when _____ receive electrical energy

and emit _____.

B. Label the *LED* and *photons* in the circuit.

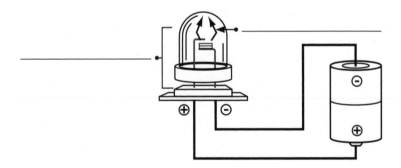

C. Read each sentence. Cross out the word that makes the sentence false and replace it with a word that makes the sentence true.

1. LEDs convert electrical energy into heat energy.

2. Excited electrons release light energy in the form of circuits.

3. An LED is less efficient than an ordinary light bulb.

Daily Science

Big Idea 5

Electrical energy can be converted into heat, light, sound, and motion.

Week 3
How do hearing aids help people hear?

An estimated 28 million people in the United States suffer from some form of hearing loss, but health researchers think that only 20% of these people use hearing aids. This week, students learn how hearing aids work. Hearing aids consist of a microphone that receives sound waves and circuitry that converts the sound waves into an electric signal. An amplifier strengthens the signal and sends it to the speaker, which then converts the electric signal back into sound waves that are broadcast directly into the ear canal of the wearer.

Day One

Vocabulary: *hearing aid, sound waves*

Materials: page 141

Begin the lesson by introducing the vocabulary and explaining, if necessary, what sound waves are and how they travel. (vibrations that contract and expand the molecules around them, much like the way a spring contracts and expands) After students have read the passage, have them complete the activities. Review the answers together.

Day Two

Vocabulary: *amplifier, microphone, speaker*

Materials: page 142

Introduce the vocabulary, pointing out each part on the diagram. Explain that the amplifier is part of the circuit in a hearing aid and isn't as easily recognizable as the speaker, microphone, or battery can be. Then have students read the passage and complete the activities. Review the answers together.

Day Three

Vocabulary: *electromagnet*

Materials: page 143

Begin by reviewing what an electromagnet is, what a permanent magnet is, and how they work. (*permanent magnet*: a magnet that always has a magnetic field, e.g., a refrigerator magnet; *electromagnet*: metal wrapped in wire that becomes a magnet when electric current flows through the wire) After students have finished reading, direct them to complete the activities. Review the answers together.

Day Four

Materials: page 144

Ask students if anyone has direct experience with a hearing aid, either worn by themselves or by a relative. Invite volunteers to share their knowledge about the hearing aid (what it looks like, what it feels like to wear, etc.). After students read the passage, direct them to complete the activities. Invite students to share what they wrote for activity B.

Day Five

Materials: page 145

Have students complete the page independently. Then review the answers together.

Daily Science • EMC 5014 • © Evan-Moor Corp.

Name _____

Day 1

Weekly Question

How do hearing aids help people hear?

When our ears are healthy and working properly, **sound waves** are collected by the outer ear, vibrate special bones in the middle ear, and travel to the inner ear. These vibrations send a signal that our brain interprets as sound. But sometimes an injury or a disease can damage parts of the ear so that we don't hear sound properly. In fact, there are 28 million people in the U.S. who suffer from hearing loss. These people can often hear better by using a **hearing aid**. Hearing aids use electricity to help our ears better recognize sounds.

Vocabulary

hearing aid
HEER-ing ayd
an electronic device that uses electricity to help the ear hear sounds better

sound waves
sownd wayvz
waves of energy created when an object moves back and forth rapidly

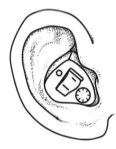 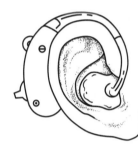

Some hearing aids fit inside the ear, while others sit behind it.

A. Use the vocabulary words to complete the paragraph.

When people have hearing loss, they can use a

_____ to help them hear. The earliest

hearing aids were shaped like horns. These horns helped

focus _____ into people's ears.

B. Write *true* or *false*.

1. Hearing aids contribute to hearing loss. _____

2. Special parts in our ears vibrate when sound reaches them. _____

3. Hearing aids use electricity to help our ears hear sounds. _____

Name _____

Modern hearing aids have four main parts: a battery, a **microphone**, an **amplifier**, and a **speaker**. The battery powers the hearing aid. The microphone works by receiving sound waves and changing the vibrations into electric current. The electric current then travels through a circuit in the hearing aid, where it is made stronger by the amplifier. The amplifier sends the stronger current to the speaker, which changes the current back into sound waves. These sound waves then travel into the middle ear or sometimes directly to the inner ear.

Vocabulary

amplifier
AM-plih-fy-ur
a device that increases electric current

microphone
MY-kroh-fone
a device that converts sound waves into electric current

speaker
SPEE-kur
a device that converts electric current into sound waves

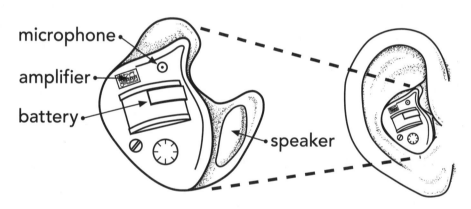

microphone
amplifier
battery
speaker

A. Number the steps in the correct order to describe how a hearing aid works.

_____ The sound waves are transmitted to the inner ear.

_____ The amplifier increases the strength of the electric current.

_____ The microphone transforms sound waves into electric current.

_____ The microphone receives sound waves.

_____ The speaker converts electric current into sound waves.

B. Most hearing aids have a control for the volume. Why do you think that is?

_____

_____

Name _____

Day 3

Weekly Question

How do hearing aids help people hear?

Both microphones and speakers use magnets and electricity to work. When a microphone receives sound waves, part of it vibrates and pushes a metal coil back and forth quickly over a permanent magnet. This is what changes sound waves into electric current. Then the amplifier makes the current stronger before it travels to the speaker. When the current reaches the speaker, an **electromagnet** turns on and off quickly, creating a changing magnetic field. These pulses in the magnetic field cause the speaker to vibrate and produce new, stronger sound waves.

Vocabulary

electromagnet
ee-LEK-troh-MAG-net
a magnet created by electric current flowing through a wire coil

A. Look at the illustrations. Label the *microphone* and the *speaker*.

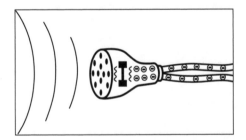   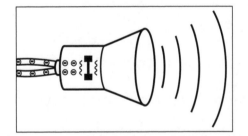

_____   _____

B. Use *microphone*, *speaker*, or *amplifier* to answer each question.

1. Which part of a hearing aid creates electric current?   _____

2. Which part of a hearing aid uses an electromagnet?   _____

3. Which part of a hearing aid uses a permanent magnet?   _____

4. Which part of a hearing aid makes the electric current stronger?   _____

Name _____

How do hearing aids help people hear?

Daily Science

Big Idea 5

WEEK 3

Although most hearing aids have the same parts, there are different types of hearing aids. One type, called a telecoil, has a metal coil instead of a microphone. Another type of hearing aid, called a digital hearing aid, converts the sound waves into electronic data, the same way music is converted into electronic data in a CD or MP3 player. This kind of hearing aid then translates the data into an electronic signal that is sent to the hearing aid's speaker.

Regardless of the type of hearing aid, they all convert electrical energy into sound waves. And while no hearing aid works as well as a healthy set of ears, hearing aids do make it possible for millions of people to hear better.

A. Write *true* or *false*.

1. Digital hearing aids convert sound waves into data. _____

2. All hearing aids convert electricity into sound waves. _____

3. Hearing aids often work better than healthy ears do. _____

4. Most hearing aids have few parts in common. _____

B. Sound amplifiers are not only used for hearing aids. Name three other devices that you can think of that might use sound amplifiers.

1. _____

2. _____

3. _____

Name _____

Day 5 *Weekly Question*

How do hearing aids help people hear?

A. Use the words in the box to complete the paragraph.

> microphone electromagnet amplifier
> hearing aid sound waves speaker

A _____ is a device that receives and sends

_____. The _____ in a hearing

aid receives sound waves and turns them into electricity. The

_____ makes the electric current stronger. The current

travels to an _____ inside the _____,

where the electricity becomes new, stronger sound waves.

B. Look at the diagram. Label the *microphone* and *speaker*. Then write
a caption that explains how sound waves travel through a hearing aid.

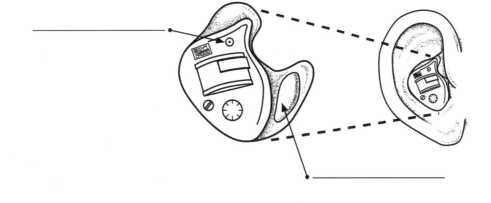

_____

_____

_____

Electrical energy can be converted into heat, light, sound, and motion.

Week 4
How do electric cars work?

Electric cars run by using batteries and electric motors. This week, students learn that electrical energy flows from the battery to the electric motor, where opposing magnetic forces between a permanent magnet and an electromagnet cause a rod to spin. This interaction converts electrical energy into mechanical energy and makes the wheels of a car turn. Students also learn about a device called the controller, which helps speed up and slow down an electric car. Finally, students discover that the same principle of conversion of electrical energy into mechanical energy is at work in familiar machines they use every day.

Day One

Vocabulary: *electric motor, mechanical energy*

Materials: page 147

Discuss with students what they know about how vehicles are powered. (gasoline, diesel fuel, electricity, hybrid) Tell students that this week they will learn how electricity can power cars. After introducing the vocabulary, have students read the passage and complete the activities. Review the answers together.

Day Two

Vocabulary: *electromagnet, magnetic force*

Materials: page 148; pair of magnets

If necessary, review with students how an electromagnet works prior to beginning the lesson. (An electric current runs through a coil of wire around an iron rod, which creates a magnetic field.) Introduce the vocabulary word and use two magnets to demonstrate how they can attract or repel each other. After students read the passage, have them complete the activities. Review the answers together.

Day Three

Vocabulary: *controller*

Materials: page 149; electric fan (optional)

Begin the lesson by explaining that electric motors can run at different speeds. If possible, use an electric fan to demonstrate how it can change speeds, and point out that the buttons on the fan control how fast the motor spins. Then introduce the vocabulary word. After students read the passage, have them complete the activities. Review the answers together.

Day Four

Materials: page 150

Remind students that electric cars are not the only devices that turn electrical energy into mechanical energy. After students read the passage, direct them to complete the activity. You may wish to complete part of the chart as a class. Review the answers together.

Day Five

Materials: page 151

Have students complete the page independently. Then review the answers together.

   Daily Science • EMC 5014 • © Evan-Moor Corp.

Name _____

Day 1

Weekly Question

How do electric cars work?

You use electrical energy every day to run your TV, computer, music player, and lots of other devices. But it took scientists a while to figure out a good way to make a car move quickly and for a long period of time by using electricity. Until fairly recently, almost all cars used gasoline. Today, many cars run on both electricity and gas. And some cars run entirely on electricity.

Most electric cars look just like regular cars on the outside, but under the hood they are very different. In an electric car, batteries generate electrical energy that is conducted through a circuit to an **electric motor**. The electric motor converts electricity from the batteries into **mechanical energy**, the energy of motion. This is what causes the wheels of the car to turn.

Vocabulary

electric motor
ee-LEK-trik
MOW-tur
a device that converts electrical energy into mechanical energy

mechanical energy
meh-KAN-ih-kull
EN-ur-gee
a form of energy expressed as motion

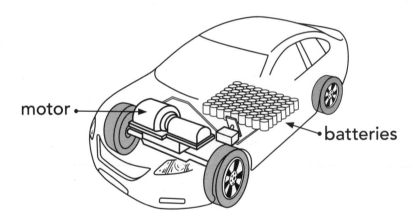

motor

batteries

A. Complete the analogy.

Gasoline is to *gas-powered car* as *battery* is to _____.

B. Use information from the passage to complete the sentences.

1. The _____ converts electricity into _____.

2. In an electric car, _____ generate electricity.

3. Mechanical energy can also be called _____.

Name _____

Day 2

Weekly Question

How do electric cars work?

How does an electric motor convert electricity into mechanical energy? Electric current flows through a coil of wire wrapped around a metal frame. This causes the frame to become an electromagnet. The electromagnet is surrounded by a permanent magnet. The two **magnetic forces** push and pull against each other, making a rod in the middle of the frame spin. That rod is connected to the wheels of a car, and when it rotates, the wheels turn and your car moves.

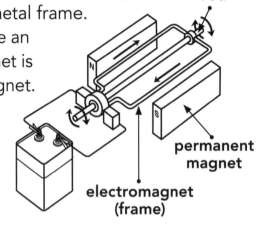

rod

permanent magnet

electromagnet (frame)

Inside an electric motor

Vocabulary

magnetic force
mag-NEH-tik forss
the force produced by a magnet that can attract or push away other magnets

A. Complete the sentence that describes how an electric motor creates mechanical energy.

The _____ between the permanent

magnet and the _____ inside the motor

cause the rod to spin.

B. Number the events in the correct order to explain how electricity makes a car move.

____ The coil and frame become an electromagnet.

____ The wheels turn.

____ The electromagnet spins.

____ Electric current flows through a wire wrapped around a frame.

____ The electromagnet pushes and pulls against a permanent magnet.

Name _____

Day 3

Weekly Question

How do electric cars work?

When a person is driving an electric car, he or she can speed up or slow down the car with the help of a device called a **controller**. The controller is located between the car batteries and the electric motor and is connected to a pedal inside the car. When the driver presses down on the pedal, the pedal sends a signal to the controller. The controller then delivers a certain amount of electric current to the electric motor, depending on how far down the driver presses the pedal. The farther down the driver presses the pedal, the more electricity the controller sends to the motor. The more current that is sent to the electric motor, the faster the car goes.

Vocabulary

controller
kun-TROL-er
a device in an electric car that regulates the amount of electric current sent from the battery to the motor

A. Write the number of each description next to the part of the electric car that it describes.

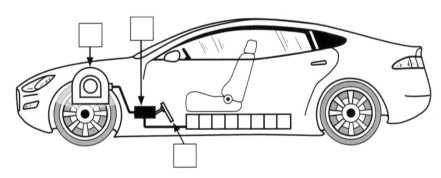

1. This part is used by the driver to send a signal to the controller.

2. This part spins based on how much electric current it receives.

3. This part sends electric current to the motor.

B. When the controller sends electric current to the motor, it causes the rod connected to the wheels to spin. Why would sending more current make the car go faster?

_____

Name _____

Day 4

Weekly Question

How do electric cars work?

Think about how your life would be different without cars, airplanes, refrigerators, or computers. All these inventions that make our lives so much easier are fairly recent. And they all depend on electric motors. The source of electricity for the motor can be a battery or an electric current generated in a power plant and delivered to your home through wires. But all electric motors are alike in that they use electrical energy and magnetic force to produce mechanical energy. If something uses electricity and has a part that spins, it probably has a motor.

All the items in the chart have electric motors. Visualize each device. Then complete the chart.

Machine	Source of electricity (*outlet* or *battery*)	Which parts move?
Blender		
Clothes washer		
Electric toothbrush		
Electric mixer		
Remote-control car		
Electric fan		

Name _____

Day 5

Weekly Question

How do electric cars work?

A. Use the words in the box to complete the sentences.

> electromagnet   mechanical energy   controller
> electric motor   magnetic force

1. Electrical energy is converted into _____ in the

_____ of an electric car.

2. When a driver presses down on the pedal, a _____

delivers the right amount of electric current to the motor.

3. An _____ and a permanent magnet both

have _____.

B. Label the *permanent magnet* and the *electromagnet* in the motor.

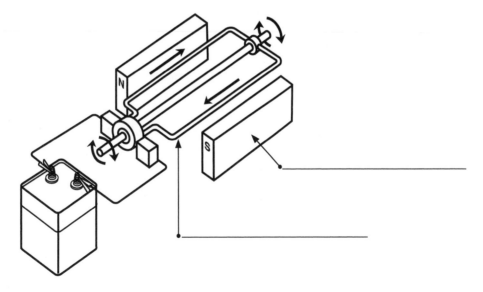

Name _____

Unit Review

Comprehension
Electrical Energy

Daily Science
Big Idea 5

WEEK 5

Fill in the bubble next to the correct answer.

1. The filament in a toaster acts like a _____ and changes some of the electrical energy into _____.

   Ⓐ resistor, heat   Ⓒ battery, light

   Ⓑ conductor, heat   Ⓓ circuit, light

2. What does electric current change into after it passes through an LED?

   Ⓐ electrons   Ⓒ heat

   Ⓑ segments   Ⓓ photons

3. Which machine does NOT use an electromagnet?

   Ⓐ LED   Ⓒ hearing aid

   Ⓑ electric motor   Ⓓ electric car

4. In a hearing aid, electrical energy is changed into _____.

   Ⓐ heat waves   Ⓒ sound waves

   Ⓑ light energy   Ⓓ mechanical energy

5. An electric motor changes electrical energy into _____.

   Ⓐ heat energy   Ⓒ light energy

   Ⓑ mechanical energy   Ⓓ sound energy

6. The source of electricity for an electric car is a _____.

   Ⓐ circuit   Ⓒ battery

   Ⓑ resistor   Ⓓ LED

Name _____

Unit Review *Vocabulary*

Word Energizer

Next to each vocabulary word, write the letter of its definition.

_____ **1.** circuit

_____ **2.** conductor

_____ **3.** electric current

_____ **4.** electric motor

_____ **5.** electromagnet

_____ **6.** electron

_____ **7.** filaments

_____ **8.** LED

_____ **9.** magnetic force

_____ **10.** mechanical energy

_____ **11.** microphone

_____ **12.** photon

_____ **13.** radiate

_____ **14.** resistor

_____ **15.** sound waves

_____ **16.** speaker

_____ **17.** switch

a. the flow of electricity

b. a particle of an atom with a negative charge

c. part of a circuit that starts or stops the flow of electric current

d. something that allows electric current to flow easily

e. something that limits the flow of electric current

f. wires that heat up when they conduct electricity

g. to send out energy in waves or rays

h. a device that converts electrical energy into light

i. a path along which an electric current flows

j. a tiny unit of light energy

k. waves of energy created by vibration

l. a device that converts sound waves into electric current

m. a device that converts electric current into sound waves

n. a magnet created by electricity flowing through a wire coiled around an iron core

o. a device that changes electrical energy into mechanical energy

p. the energy of motion

q. a force that attracts or pushes away other magnets

Name _____

Unit Review

Visual Literacy

Kinds of Energy

For each picture, list the kind or kinds of energy that are being converted from electrical energy (*heat*, *light*, *sound*, or *motion*).

1.

_____

2.

_____

3.

_____

4.

_____

5.

_____

6.

_____

7.

_____

Daily Science • EMC 5014 • © Evan-Moor Corp.

Name _____

Unit Review

Hands-on Activity
Start Your Motor

When you think about an electric motor, you might imagine a complex machine with many moving parts. But, in fact, you can create your own electric motor using a permanent magnet and an electromagnet.

What You Need

- flat-head metal screw
- disc magnet
- 6 inches of copper wire
- 1.5-volt C battery

1. Set the flat head of the metal screw down on top of the disc magnet.

2. Lower the battery so that it touches the tip of the screw.

3. Lift up the battery.

4. Hold one end of the wire to the top of the battery. Touch the side of the magnet with the other end of the wire.

What Did You Discover?

1. Describe what happened when you lifted up the battery.

_____

2. Describe what happened when you touched the other end of the wire to the magnet.

_____

3. Which part of the device is the electromagnet? Explain.

_____

Big Idea 6

People invented machines to make work easier.

Key Concept
Simple machines make work easier.

National Standard
People continue inventing new ways of doing things, solving problems, and getting work done.

In this unit, students learn that work is done by exerting a force over a distance. They see that simple machines make work easier, meaning that machines allow you to do work by using less force, but there is a trade-off. When you use less force to do work, you have to spread that force over a longer distance. Students will learn the following:

→ an inclined plane decreases the amount of force but increases the distance needed to do work;

→ the wedge and the screw change the direction of the force that is applied to them;

→ a pulley changes the direction of the force applied to it or changes the amount of force needed to do work; and

→ a wheelbarrow is a compound machine made up of the lever and the wheel and axle.

Teacher Background

Machines are everywhere. From buses and cars to elevators and ramps; from scissors to watches to wheelbarrows—we depend on machines to help us do our work.

All machines rely, in part, on the six simple machines: the inclined plane, the lever, the wedge, the wheel and axle, the pulley, and the screw. In fact, most machines are compound machines, which are combinations of simple machines.

Simple machines make it easier to do work by either changing the direction of force so that the force can be better used, or by multiplying the output of force. This latter effect is called mechanical advantage. Some simple machines change the direction of force, some provide mechanical advantage, and some do both.

For specific background information on each week's concepts, refer to the notes on pp. 158, 164, 170, and 176.

Unit Overview

WEEK 1: Why do some building entrances have ramps?

Connection to the Big Idea: Ramps are inclined planes, a kind of simple machine.

This week, students are introduced to simple machines and the inclined plane. They learn that the inclined plane makes work easier. To understand this, students learn how scientists define work, and how force and distance are combined to do work.

Content Vocabulary: *distance, force, inclined plane, simple machine, work*

WEEK 2: What's the difference between a nail and a screw?

Connection to the Big Idea: Screws and wedges are simple machines.

This week, students learn that the screw and wedge are simple machines that change the direction of the force applied to them.

Content Vocabulary: *friction, screw, threads, wedge*

WEEK 3: How do elevators work?

Connection to the Big Idea: Elevators have pulleys, which are a simple machine.

This week, students learn about the pulley. They learn that a fixed pulley changes the direction of force, while a movable pulley reduces the amount of force needed to do work, also called mechanical advantage. Students then learn that elevators use a counterweight to help lift or lower the car.

Content Vocabulary: *counterweight, fixed pulley, load, mechanical advantage, movable pulley, pulley*

WEEK 4: How does a wheelbarrow make work easier?

Connection to the Big Idea: A wheelbarrow is a compound machine made up of the lever and the wheel and axle.

Students learn that a wheelbarrow is a compound machine made up of the lever and a wheel and axle. The lever in a wheelbarrow makes it easier to lift or lower the load, and the wheel and axle overcome friction to let the wheelbarrow roll.

Content Vocabulary: *compound machine, fulcrum, lever, wheel and axle, wheelbarrow*

WEEK 5: Unit Review

You may choose to do these activities to review concepts of simple machines.

p. 182: Comprehension Students answer multiple-choice items about key concepts of the unit.

p. 183: Vocabulary Students complete a crossword puzzle to show that they understand unit vocabulary.

p. 184: Visual Literacy Students identify the simple machines that make up some common compound machines.

p. 185: Hands-on Activity Students experiment with levers to see how moving the fulcrum changes how much force is needed to lift an object. Review the materials and instructions on the student page ahead of time.

People invented machines to make work easier.

Week 1
Why do some building entrances have ramps?

This week's lessons build on students' familiarity with ramps at building entrances to discuss inclined planes and how they make doing work easier. Students will likely need help understanding that the scientific definition of *work*—the use of force to move something over distance—has nothing to do with effort. Depending on your students' ability levels, you may wish to introduce them to the scientific formula used to calculate work: Work = Force x Distance (W = F x D).

Day One

Vocabulary: *inclined plane, simple machine*

Materials: page 159

Direct students' attention to the illustration on the page. Ask them to point out the ramp and to speculate what the ramp is for. (to help people get into buildings) Tell students that a ramp is an example of an inclined plane, which is one of the six simple machines. Introduce the vocabulary, have students complete the page, and then go over the answers together.

Day Two

Vocabulary: *distance, force, work*

Materials: page 160

Because students will likely think that "work" is the same as "effort," take time to use the vocabulary words *force* and *distance* to explain what work is in scientific terms (the use of force to move something over a certain distance). Students may benefit from doing the page as a group.

Day Three

Materials: page 161; heavy book, measuring tape or yardstick, and board or other inclined plane

Have students take turns lifting the heavy book and then pushing it up the inclined plane, measuring the distance the book was lifted versus slid up the inclined plane. When students have completed activity A, review the answers together. Then review the concept of *work* by asking: *Who did more work, Marco or Maria?* (They both did the same amount of work.) *Why is that?* (They both moved their bowling balls to the same place.)

Day Four

Materials: page 162

If students have trouble thinking of places to list in activity A, consider doing the activity as a group. If necessary, review the concept of *gravity* (the natural force that pulls everything to Earth's center) before students complete activity B. You may also wish to explain that the ladder is an inclined plane, because it is tilted at an angle. It would be easier to climb than a ladder that is not tilted. Then review the answers together.

Day Five

Materials: page 163

Have students complete the page independently. Then review the answers together.

Daily Science • EMC 5014 • © Evan-Moor Corp.

Name _____

Day 1

Weekly Question

Why do some building entrances have ramps?

If a building has stairs at the entrance, it probably has a long ramp leading to the door, too. That ramp is an example of an **inclined plane**. One end of an inclined plane is higher than the other. Inclined planes are everywhere. Ramps, playground slides, and ladders are examples of inclined planes. An inclined plane is a **simple machine**. Simple machines are tools that help you do work.

MONTE VISTA SCHOOL

Vocabulary

inclined plane
in-KLINED playn
a flat surface that is tilted at an angle

simple machine
SIM-pull muh-SHEEN
a basic tool that makes work easier to do and has few or no moving parts

A. Complete the analogy.

Inclined plane is to *simple machine* as _____.

☐ *ramp* is to *stairs* ☐ *triangle* is to *shape* ☐ *nails* are to *hammer*

B. Which object in each pair is an *inclined plane*? Write the word or words.

1. a ramp or a table _____

2. a swing set or a slide _____

3. a ladder or a hammer _____

4. an escalator or an elevator _____

5. a trail up a hill or a flat sidewalk _____

Name _____

If simple machines help you do work, then what do we mean exactly when we say "work"? Scientists say that **work** is the **force** applied to an object to move it a certain **distance**. When you walk up stairs or along a ramp, you are doing work. You are applying force to move yourself a distance. Scientists don't measure work just by how much force you use or how far a distance you travel. They look at the end result. So whether you use stairs or a ramp to reach the entrance, the amount of work you are doing is the same. You are using less force over a greater distance or more force over a shorter distance.

A. Check the box next to the caption that correctly describes what is happening in the picture.

LIBRARY

☐ The person using the stairs is doing more work.

☐ Both people are doing the same amount of work.

☐ The person using the ramp is doing more work.

B. Use the vocabulary words to complete the sentences.

1. Lifting and tugging are examples of _____ being applied.

2. The _____ between two places can be measured in inches, feet, or miles.

3. An inclined plane makes it easier for you to do _____.

Vocabulary

distance
DIS-tinss
the amount of space between two points

force
forss
a push or pull that can change the position of an object

work
werk
the use of force to move something over a distance

Name _____

Day 3

Weekly Question

Why do some building entrances have ramps?

An inclined plane makes work easier to accomplish by reducing the amount of force you must use to move something. But there's a trade-off. When you use less force to do work, you have to increase the distance. If you lift a heavy box up to a shelf five feet in the air, the distance is five feet. If you push a box up a ten-foot ramp to the same shelf, the distance is ten feet. The box ends up in the same place. But when you push the box up the ramp, you are using less force over a longer distance. The force you exert is smaller.

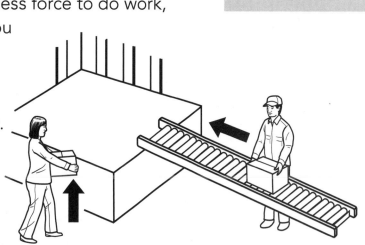

A. Read the sentences. Then answer the questions.

Marco lifts his bowling ball up to a shelf that is three feet high. His sister, Maria, uses an inclined plane that is five feet long to roll her bowling ball up to the same shelf.

1. Who used more force? _____

2. Who moved the ball a longer distance? _____

B. Look at the two inclined planes below. Check the box next to the ramp that requires more force to move things up it. Explain your answer.

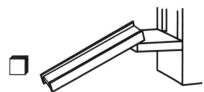 

_____

Name _____

Day 4

Weekly Question

Why do some building entrances have ramps?

Daily Science

Big Idea 6

WEEK 1

Because they are inclined planes, ramps in front of building entrances require less force to go up them than stairs do. This means that people in wheelchairs or people who have difficulty walking can use the ramps to get into buildings. People can also push or carry heavy objects into buildings more easily. Ramps are important because they give everyone access to places such as schools, restaurants, and other public buildings.

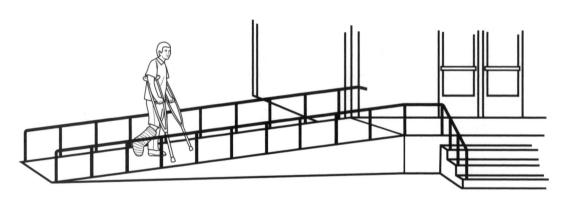

A. Name four places you have been to that have a ramp in front of them.

1. _____ 3. _____

2. _____ 4. _____

B. Look at the drawing of a slide. Circle the two inclined planes in the picture. Then answer the questions.

1. Which inclined plane requires you to use force? _____

2. Which inclined plane uses the force of gravity to do work? _____

Name _____

Day 5

Weekly Question

Why do some building entrances have ramps?

Daily Science
Big Idea 6

WEEK 1

A. Use the words in the box to complete the paragraph.

> force　inclined plane　distance
> work　simple machine

Chandra needed to carry a heavy box up a flight of stairs. To make

the _____ require less effort, she made a ramp. This

ramp, or _____, was a board that she laid over the steps.

It was an example of a _____. The _____

from the bottom of the ramp to the top was ten feet. Chandra applied

_____ and moved the box up the ramp.

B. Check the box below the ramp that makes it easier to move the piano.

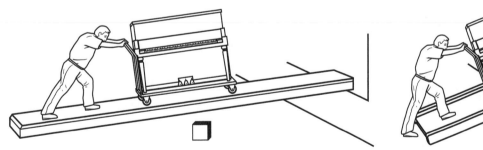

C. In your own words, explain how inclined planes make work easier.

_____

_____

Big Idea 6

People invented machines to make work easier.

Week 2
What's the difference between a nail and a screw?

This week, students increase their understanding of simple machines by learning the difference between nails and screws. Both nails and screws change the direction of the force applied to them, but they differ in how they do this. A screw uses a rotational force. When the screw turns, that force becomes motion along a straight line. A nail, on the other hand, is a kind of wedge. When you hammer a nail, the force starts off traveling in one direction. But some of this force gets redirected sideways, which is why a wedge can split or push away the material into which it is driven.

Day One

Vocabulary: *screw, wedge*

Materials: page 165; variety of nails and screws

Allow students to examine the collection of nails and screws and to make observations about the similarities and differences between them. (e.g., length, width, threads versus smooth sides) Inform students that both a nail and a screw are simple machines, and that this week they will learn about how these simple machines operate. After students have finished reading the passage, complete activity A together and ask volunteers to share their predictions and explain their thinking. Direct students to complete activity B independently.

Day Two

Materials: page 166; nails, hammer, piece of wood

After students have read the passage, have them examine the nails and name the parts. (pole, wedge) Use the hammer to drive a nail into the wood. Then ask students to find the part of the passage that explains what happened. (paragraph 2, sentences 2 through 4) After students have completed the activities, go over the answers together.

Day Three

Vocabulary: *threads*

Materials: page 167

Review how a nail changes the direction of force. Tell students that a screw changes the force applied to it in a different way. Read the passage and do the activities together to ensure understanding.

Day Four

Vocabulary: *friction*

Materials: page 168; 2 pieces of sandpaper

After introducing the vocabulary word, help students understand friction by asking volunteers to rub the pieces of sandpaper together. Ask: *Can you feel the resistance to movement?* Then direct students to read the first paragraph to find out what friction has to do with nails and screws. Explain that the next paragraph sums up the answer to the week's question. You may wish to do the activities together to help students summarize the concepts.

Day Five

Materials: page 169

Have students complete the page independently. Then review the answers together.

Name _____

Weekly Question

What's the difference between a nail and a screw?

Daily Science
Big Idea 6

WEEK 2

If you've ever looked inside a messy toolbox, you've probably found nails and screws mixed together. Both are tools that help us hold things in place. A nail is an example of a simple machine called a **wedge**. A **screw** is another type of simple machine. Remember that simple machines help us do work, and that work is the use of force to move something a certain distance. When you use a wedge or a screw, the force that you apply changes direction.

A. Look at the pictures. Then follow the directions.

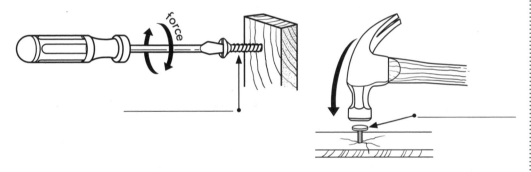

1. Use the vocabulary words to label each simple machine.

2. Draw arrows to show how you think the direction of the force being applied to each simple machine might change.

B. Use words from the passage to complete the sentences.

1. A circular force is applied to a _____.

2. A nail is an example of a _____.

3. Screws and wedges are _____.

4. When you apply force to a nail or a screw,

   the force _____.

Vocabulary

screw
skroo
a simple machine that changes a circular force to an up-or-down force

wedge
wej
a simple machine, such as a nail or an ax, that changes the angle and direction of force

Name _____

Day 2

Weekly Question

What's the difference between a nail and a screw?

All wedges have a wide end and a narrow end that comes to a point. When you apply force to the wide end, it travels through the wedge to the narrow end. But as this force travels, something happens. The force splits into different directions. Part of the force is directed sideways to push things out of its way. This is why wedges, such as axes and knives, are able to split things apart.

A nail is a pole with a wedge at the tip. When you hit a nail with a hammer, the force travels through the pole to the wedge, and some of the force changes direction. The force that changes direction pushes the wood out of the way. The other part of the force moves the nail deeper into the wood.

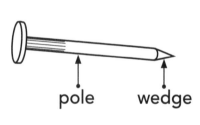

pole   wedge

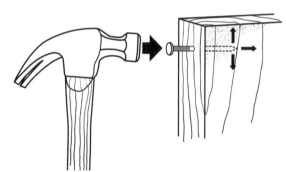

A. All wedges push something out of the way when the force changes direction. Next to each of these wedges, write what is pushed out of the way.

1. shovel _____

3. your teeth _____

2. sewing needle _____

4. ax _____

B. When you hit a nail with a hammer, why does the nail go into the wood? Explain in your own words.

_____

_____

Name _____

Weekly Question

Day 3 What's the difference between a nail and a screw?

When you use a screwdriver, you turn a screw clockwise (down) or counterclockwise (up). The **threads** on a screw change the direction of the force to move the screw forward or backward.

A screw's threads are actually an inclined plane wrapped around a pole. So the whole screw works like an inclined plane. It allows you to use less force to move the screw. The trade-off is that you have to turn a screw many times to move it forward (down) or backward (up).

Vocabulary

threads
thredz
the grooved, or spiral, edge twisted around the pole of a screw

A. If you could take apart a screw, it would look something like the illustration below. Use information from the passage to label the parts of the screw.

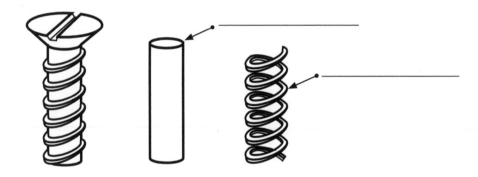

B. Complete the analogy.

Nail is to *wedge* as *screw* is to _____.

☐ pole   ☐ inclined plane   ☐ screwdriver

C. If you turn a screwdriver one direction and the screw goes into the wood, what will happen if you turn the screwdriver the other direction?

_____

Name _____

What's the difference between a nail and a screw?

Both screws and nails are used to hold things in place. This works because of the **friction** between a nail or screw and the surface it is attached to. Long, thick nails or screws will create more friction than short, thin nails or screws. So longer, thicker nails and screws are best for keeping heavy things in place.

The biggest difference between a nail and a screw is how each tool changes the force we apply to it. Because a nail is a kind of wedge, some of the downward force of the hammer goes sideways. A screw, on the other hand, starts with a force that is applied by turning. The threads on a screw turn circular force into forward or backward force. But both the wedge and the screw change the direction of the force to make work easier.

Vocabulary

friction
FRIK-shun
the resistance to movement caused when two surfaces touch

A. Why do long, thick nails hold up heavier objects better than short, thin nails do?

_____

_____

B. List two similarities between a nail and a screw.

1. _____

2. _____

C. List two differences between a nail and a screw.

1. _____

2. _____

Name _____

Day 5

Weekly Question

What's the difference between a nail and a screw?

Daily Science

Big Idea 6

WEEK 2

A. Use the words in the box to complete the sentences.

> screw   wedge   friction   threads

1. A knife is an example of a _____.

2. The _____ on a screw are an inclined plane.

3. You apply circular force to a _____.

4. Nails and screws use the force of _____ to hold things in place.

B. Write *true* or *false*.

1. Both nails and screws have a pole. _____

2. The same direction of force is applied to both a nail and a screw. _____

3. A hammer is used to apply force to a screw. _____

4. A wedge can change downward force to sideways force. _____

C. Write whether each object uses a *screw* or a *wedge*.

_____   _____   _____   _____   _____

Big Idea 6

People invented machines to make work easier.

Week 3
How do elevators work?

This week, students are introduced to another simple machine, the pulley. Pulleys are wheels with grooves that hold ropes or cables. The grooves keep the rope or cable from slipping off the pulley. A pulley can either be fixed or movable. Fixed pulleys, like those used in elevators, change the direction of the force that is applied to them. They are used to lift and lower objects. Movable pulleys travel with the load. They provide mechanical advantage, which means that they make it easier to lift or lower a load.

Day One

Vocabulary: *load, pulley*

Materials: page 171

Begin by asking students to guess when elevators were invented. Record their guesses on the board. Then introduce the vocabulary and have students read the passage. When students have finished, explain that the pulley, like all simple machines, is very old. Then have students complete the activities. Review the answers together, and direct students to locate information from the passage that supports their answers. For the oral activity, pair students or discuss it as a group.

Day Two

Vocabulary: *fixed pulley*

Materials: page 172

Introduce the vocabulary word and explain that a fixed pulley is fixed in place, so it does not move. If students are having trouble with activity C, prompt them to think about what the two situations have in common. (reaching a place you can't get to)

Day Three

Vocabulary: *mechanical advantage, movable pulley*

Materials: page 173

Introduce the vocabulary. Inform students that *mechanical advantage* means that the amount of force needed to do work is reduced, and that scientists use different formulas to measure the mechanical advantage that different machines provide. Tell students that in a pulley system, each movable pulley further reduces the amount of force needed to do work, making it easy to lift heavy objects. Then do the activity together as a group. If students are having trouble with item 3, provide them with some examples of movable pulleys. (e.g., cranes, flag raisers)

Day Four

Vocabulary: *counterweight*

Materials: page 174

Introduce the vocabulary word and instruct students to look at the diagram before they read the passage and complete the activity. When students have finished, review the answers together. Ask individuals to explain in their own words the action indicated in the drawing. (e.g., The motor turns the pulley and the car lifts or lowers while the weight lowers or lifts.)

Day Five

Materials: page 175

Have students complete the page independently. Then go over answers together.

Name _____

Day 1

Weekly Question

How do elevators work?

The first elevator about 2,000 years ago was probably nothing more than a rope tied to a box and thrown over a branch. Today, elevators are safer, faster, and powered by electricity, but their design hasn't changed much. All elevators have a car that lifts people and things. Most elevators use **pulleys** and cables that are attached to the car.

A pulley is a simple machine. It is a wheel with a deep groove in it. A rope or cable fits into the groove. Pulleys can change the direction of force, the amount of force needed, or both the direction and the amount of force to lift and lower a **load**.

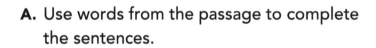

Vocabulary

load
lohd
something that is carried or moved

pulley
PULL-ee
a simple machine made of a wheel with a grooved rim over which a rope or cable is looped

A. Use words from the passage to complete the sentences.

1. The _____ is a simple machine.

2. A pulley is made of a _____ that has

   a _____ for rope or cable.

3. Today's _____ are powered by electricity.

B. Write *true* or *false*.

1. An elevator uses a pulley and a cable to move a car. _____

2. A pulley is a simple machine. _____

3. Pulleys can change only the direction of force. _____

 Talk

According to the passage, how is a pulley like an inclined plane? How is it like a screw? Tell a partner.

Name _____

Weekly Question

How do elevators work?

The pulley that elevators use is called a **fixed pulley**. A fixed pulley doesn't change the amount of force you need to do work, but it does change the direction of that force. A pulley rotates, or turns, the force. When you pull down, the pulley changes the direction of the force to lift the load up. Fixed pulleys help us do work, because people find it easier to pull down than to lift up. Pulleys can also help us lift or lower things that might be too high or too low for people to reach by themselves.

Vocabulary

fixed pulley
fixt PULL-ee
a pulley that is attached to something and does not move

A. Draw arrows to show how a pulley changes the direction of force.

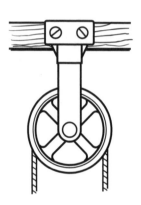

B. Write *true* or *false*.

1. Fixed pulleys are pulleys that stay in place.

_____

2. A fixed pulley reduces the amount of force you need to do work.

_____

3. A fixed pulley is best used for lifting or lowering things too heavy to lift by yourself.

_____

C. If a fixed pulley doesn't change the amount of force you use to do work, how might a pulley be good to do the following?

1. raise a flag _____

2. lower a bucket into a well _____

_____

Name _____

Day 3

Weekly Question

How do elevators work?

Daily Science

Big Idea 6

WEEK 3

Not all pulleys are fixed in place. Some pulleys move with the load they are lifting or lowering. These pulleys, called **movable pulleys**, reduce the amount of force you need to do the work, just like some other simple machines do. We can measure that change in the amount of force needed. When a machine allows you to do work with less force, it provides **mechanical advantage**.

Fixed pulleys and movable pulleys can be used together in pulley systems. Every time you add another movable pulley to a pulley system, you increase the mechanical advantage. But remember, there's a trade-off. You can't decrease the amount of force you need to do the work without increasing the distance. For pulleys, this means you need a lot of rope!

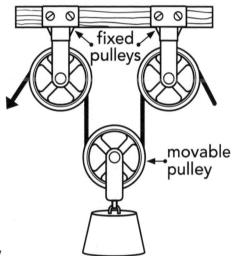

fixed pulleys

movable pulley

Vocabulary

mechanical advantage
meh-KAN-ih-kul ad-VAN-tej
the number of times a machine multiplies the force put into it

movable pulley
MOO-vuh-bul PULL-ee
a pulley that moves with the load

Answer the questions.

1. How does mechanical advantage help you do work?

_____

2. How would you increase mechanical advantage in a pulley system?

_____

3. A zip line is used to move a person or an object across a gap between high places. Why do you think a zip line uses movable pulleys?

_____

Day 4

Weekly Question

How do elevators work?

Elevators that use pulleys also use a **counterweight** to balance the weight of the car. The cable is attached to the car on one end and the counterweight on the other end, and it passes through a pulley that is attached to an electric motor.

The counterweight weighs about the same as the car would with an average number of people in it. Gravity pulls on both the counterweight and the car, balancing them. This reduces the amount of force the electric motor needs to move the elevator. The electric motor does the least amount of work when a car has an average number of riders. With more or fewer people, the motor has to work harder to move the car and the counterweight.

Vocabulary

counterweight
KOWN-tur-WAYT
a heavy weight used to balance the weight of an elevator car

Look at the diagram of a typical elevator. Then follow the instructions.

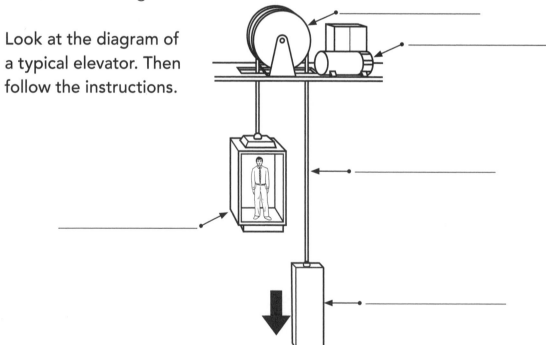

1. Using information from the passage, label the following:

   car   pulley   cable   counterweight   motor

2. Draw an arrow next to the elevator car to show the direction in which it is moving.

Name _____

Day 5

Weekly Question

How do elevators work?

A. Use the words in the box to complete the sentences.

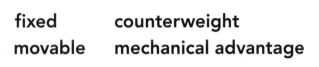

> fixed   counterweight
> movable   mechanical advantage

1. The weight of an elevator car is balanced by the _____.

2. A _____ pulley moves with the load.

3. Elevators use _____ pulleys.

4. If a machine provides _____, it allows you to use less force to do work.

B. Look at the diagram and then follow the instructions.

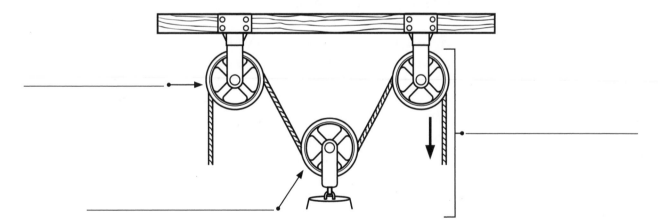

1. Label the *fixed pulley*, the *movable pulley*, and the *pulley system*.

2. Circle the pulley that provides the greatest mechanical advantage.

3. Draw an arrow next to each section of rope to show the direction in which the force on that rope is traveling.

People invented machines to make work easier.

Week 4
How does a wheelbarrow make work easier?

This week, students learn about two more simple machines, the lever and the wheel and axle, and how they work together in a wheelbarrow, which is a compound machine. The wheelbarrow is a container that is lifted and lowered by an attached lever and moved with the help of a wheel and axle. The wheelbarrow lever provides mechanical advantage, allowing a person to easily lift and lower a heavy load. The wheel overcomes friction, allowing the load to be easily moved.

Day One

Vocabulary: *lever, wheel and axle, wheelbarrow*

Materials: page 177

Review the definition of *mechanical advantage*, and tell students that this week they will learn how a wheelbarrow provides mechanical advantage. Ask how many students have used a wheelbarrow and what they've used it for. Introduce the vocabulary and explain that the wheelbarrow has two types of simple machines: the lever and the wheel and axle. Have students read the passage and complete the questions. Before students do the oral activity, discuss who uses a wheelbarrow now and whether it was used more in the past. (Since today we use motorized machines to do the heavy lifting and carrying, the wheelbarrow was used more in the past.)

Day Two

Vocabulary: *fulcrum*

Materials: page 178; ruler and eraser

Introduce the vocabulary word by placing the eraser on a desk and placing the ruler on the eraser. Point out that you have made a lever, and the eraser is the fulcrum. As students read the passage, direct their attention to the examples of each type of lever. (seesaw, wheelbarrow, fishing rod) Have students complete the activities. You may want to complete activity B as a group. Invite volunteers to share their answers.

Day Three

Materials: page 179

After students have finished reading the passage, clarify that a bicycle uses gears and chains to transfer energy from the axle to the wheel, and that a tricycle has the pedals attached directly to the wheel. Have students complete the activities. Help them to visualize the machines in activity C. Then review the answers together.

Day Four

Vocabulary: *compound machine*

Materials: page 180; scissors, can opener

After introducing students to the vocabulary word and reading the passage, direct their attention to the three illustrations of compound machines. Allow students to examine an actual pair of scissors and can opener before they complete the activities. Then discuss the answers. You may want to ask students how the tools in activity A demonstrate mechanical advantage.

Day Five

Materials: page 181

Have students complete the page independently. Then review the answers together.

Name _____

Day 1

Weekly Question

How does a wheelbarrow make work easier?

Wheelbarrows have been used in almost every culture for thousands of years. People recognized that having a container they could easily lift and move would help them do more work. Wheelbarrows provide mechanical advantage by joining a container with two simple machines. The simple machines are the **lever** and **wheel and axle**.

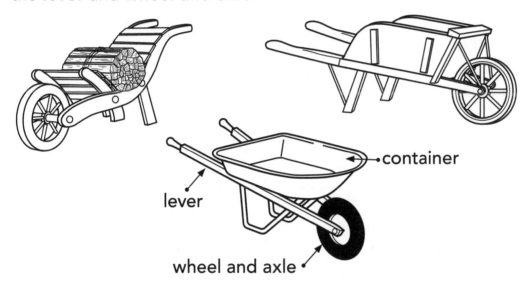

lever

wheel and axle

container

Vocabulary

lever
LEH-vur
a simple machine with a bar that allows heavy objects to be lifted or moved

wheel and axle
weel and AX-ul
a simple machine made from a wheel rotating around a fixed point

wheelbarrow
WEEL-bare-oh
a machine used for carrying heavy loads, made up of a wheel and axle, a lever, and a container

Answer the questions.

1. What are the three parts of a wheelbarrow?

   _____

2. Which parts of a wheelbarrow are simple machines?

   _____

 Talk

Who uses a wheelbarrow now? Do you think wheelbarrows are used more today or hundreds of years ago? Why do you think that? Tell a partner.

Name _____

Weekly Question
How does a wheelbarrow make work easier?

The handles on a wheelbarrow are examples of a lever. Levers are commonly used to lift a load. A lever sits on a point called the **fulcrum**. The fulcrum is where the lever pivots, or moves. On the wheelbarrow, the fulcrum is the axle of the wheel. When you push down or pull up on the handle, it pivots, or moves, on the fulcrum to raise or lower the load. The positions of the fulcrum and the load change the lever's mechanical advantage and the direction of the force.

There are three kinds of levers, depending on the positions of the force, the fulcrum, and the load.

Vocabulary

fulcrum
FULL-krum
the point of support on which a lever pivots

When the fulcrum is between you and the load, pushing down will lift the load and lifting up will lower the load.

When the load is between you and the fulcrum, the load is easier to lift or lower, but the direction of the force does not change.

When you are between the load and the fulcrum, a small movement in force causes the load to move farther.

A. Write a sentence that explains how the lever in a wheelbarrow works.

_____

_____

B. Name four examples of levers that you have seen or used.

1. _____   3. _____

2. _____   4. _____

Name _____

Day 3

Weekly Question

How does a wheelbarrow make work easier?

A wheel and axle helps you do work by changing a push or a pull into a force that rotates, or spins. With wheelbarrows, it's much easier to push a load rolling on a wheel than to drag the load along the ground.

A wheel and axle also creates mechanical advantage. When the axle rotates, the wheel moves a greater distance than the axle does. For example, when you ride a bicycle, your foot turns the pedal, which is connected to the axle. The wheel moves more than your foot does. So you contribute less force to move a greater distance than you would move if you walked.

A. Draw arrows pointing to a wheel and axle in each illustration.

B. Write *true* or *false*.

1. A wheel and axle can create mechanical advantage. _____

2. In a bicycle, the wheel moves a shorter distance when more force is applied to the pedal. _____

C. In each example below, tell whether the force applied is directed to the *wheel* or to the *axle*.

1. a faucet handle _____   3. a steering wheel _____

2. a spinning top _____   4. an airplane propeller _____

Name _____

How does a wheelbarrow make work easier?

When two or more simple machines are put together, you get a **compound machine**. Compound machines can be basic, such as a wheelbarrow or a can opener, or they can be very complex, such as a car. But even very complicated mechanical tools can be broken down into several simple machines.

Without machines, life and work would be much more difficult. Simple and compound machines make our lives better by saving us time and energy. For thousands of years, people have depended on machines. The world would not be the same without them.

Vocabulary

compound machine
KOM-pound muh-SHEEN
a combination of simple machines used to simplify tasks

A. Name the simple machines that make up each compound machine.

1. _____

2. _____

3. _____

_____

_____

_____

B. Complete the analogy.

Simple machine is to *compound machine* as _____.

☐ *nail* is to *screw*   ☐ *wheelbarrow* is to *car*

☐ *wheelbarrow* is to *lever*   ☐ *lever* is to *scissors*

Name _____

Day 5

Weekly Question

How does a wheelbarrow make work easier?

Daily Science

Big Idea 6

WEEK 4

A. Use the words in the box to complete the sentences.

> lever   wheel and axle
> fulcrum   compound machine

1. A _____ is what the lever balances on.

2. A seesaw is an example of a _____.

3. A _____ uses two or more simple machines.

4. A bike has more than one _____.

B. Answer *true* or *false*.

1. A wheelbarrow is a simple machine. _____

2. The handles of a wheelbarrow act as a lever. _____

3. A wheel and axle can change the direction of force. _____

4. It is easier to drag something than to carry it
   in a wheelbarrow. _____

C. In the left box, draw something that has a lever with a fulcrum. In the right box, draw something with a wheel and axle. Then label each simple machine.

Name _____

Fill in the bubble next to the correct answer.

1. Which of these lists contains ONLY simple machines?

    Ⓐ wedge, wheelbarrow, lever, pulley

    Ⓑ pulley, wheel and axle, screw, inclined plane

    Ⓒ lever, fulcrum, hammer, screw

    Ⓓ wheel and axle, inclined plane, scissors, wedge

2. An inclined plane requires less _____ but a greater _____ to do work.

    Ⓐ force, load   Ⓒ force, distance

    Ⓑ distance, force   Ⓓ load, distance

3. An ax is an example of a(n) _____.

    Ⓐ pulley   Ⓒ screw

    Ⓑ wedge   Ⓓ axle

4. The simple machine in an elevator is the _____.

    Ⓐ pulley   Ⓒ wedge

    Ⓑ inclined plane   Ⓓ wheel and axle

5. Mechanical advantage changes the _____.

    Ⓐ direction of force   Ⓒ simple machine being used

    Ⓑ output of force   Ⓓ amount of work being done

6. The simple machines in a wheelbarrow are _____.

    Ⓐ a lever and a pulley   Ⓒ a wheel and axle and a lever

    Ⓑ an inclined plane and a wheel   Ⓓ a lever and a wedge

Name _____

Unit Review **Vocabulary**
Puzzle It Out

Select from the list of vocabulary words to complete the puzzle.

compound machine
counterweight
distance
fixed pulley
force
friction
fulcrum
inclined plane
lever
load
mechanical advantage
movable pulley
pulley
screw
simple machine
threads
wedge
wheel and axle
wheelbarrow
work

ACROSS

1. An ax is an example of this.

4. an inclined plane wrapped around a post

7. a combination of simple machines

9. a simple machine made of a wheel with a grooved rim

10. the space between two places

11. a push or a pull that can change something's position

DOWN

1. the simple machine found on a bicycle

2. a pulley that does not move with the load

3. resistance to movement when two surfaces touch

4. one of six tools that makes work easier

5. the use of force to move a load a distance

6. A seesaw is an example of this.

8. the point on which a lever pivots or turns

Name _____

Identify the simple machines that make up each of the compound machines below.

can opener

1. _____

2. _____

3. _____

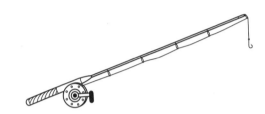

fishing pole

1. _____

2. _____

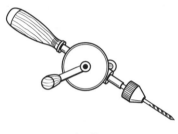

drill

1. _____

2. _____

scissors

1. _____

2. _____

shovel

1. _____

2. _____

bicycle

1. _____

2. _____

Name _____

Unit Review

Hands-on Activity

Learn About Levers

Try this simple experiment to see how the position of a fulcrum changes the amount of force you need to lift a book.

What You Need

- ruler
- block or other stable object to act as the fulcrum
- paperback book
- lightweight container such as a small plastic tub
- marbles
- masking tape

1. Assemble your lever by taping the container to the end of the ruler at the 12-inch mark.

2. Set the ruler on the fulcrum at the 6-inch mark.

3. Place the book on the end of the ruler at the 1-inch mark.

4. Add marbles to the container until the book is raised into the air.

5. Repeat step 4 with the fulcrum under the ruler at the 3-inch mark and the 9-inch mark.

What Did You Discover?

1. How many marbles did it take to lift the book when the fulcrum was at the following marks?

   3 inches: _____   6 inches: _____   9 inches: _____

2. Describe the change in force needed to lift the book when you moved the fulcrum each time.

   _____

3. Use math to figure out how many marbles it would take to lift the book if the fulcrum were at the following marks:

   4½ inches: _____   7½ inches: _____

Answer Key

Big Idea 1: Week 1 • Day 1
A. 1. true   3. false
    2. false   4. true
B. 1. dams   3. safety/shelter/
    2. deep   a hiding place
TALK: Answers will vary.

Big Idea 1: Week 1 • Day 2
A.

Answers will vary—e.g.,
The lodge walls are thick and
are made from mud, sticks,
and logs.
B. 1. lodge   3. entrance;
    2. pond   underwater
C. Answers will vary—e.g.,
Those animals can't or won't
hunt in the water.

Big Idea 1: Week 1 • Day 3
A. Beavers use logs they gather in
the summer as food during the
winter.
B. Beavers eat trees and use them
to build their lodges and dams.

Big Idea 1: Week 1 • Day 4
A. Answers will vary.

Positive Effects	Negative Effects
create new wetland habitats	destroy trees
slow soil erosion	cause silt to build up and flood the land behind them

B. 1. silt   3. wetland
    2. Erosion

Big Idea 1: Week 1 • Day 5
A. 1. silt   4. wetland
    2. habitat   5. erosion
    3. lodge
B. Dams create ponds that are
deep enough not to freeze solid
in winter.
Dams create ponds that
beavers can hide in.
C. 1. false   3. true   5. false
    2. false   4. true

Big Idea 1: Week 2 • Day 1
A. 3, 1, 4, 2
B. It would hurt the plant's ability
to spread because the plant
could not make seeds.

Big Idea 1: Week 2 • Day 2
A.

These plants are angiosperms
because they have flowers.
B. 1. angiosperms
    2. pollinate
    3. pollinators/bees/insects
C. Flowers attract pollinators.
When flowers are pollinated,
they produce fruit and seeds to
make new angiosperms.

Big Idea 1: Week 2 • Day 3
A. 1. seeds   3. scatter
    2. digestive   4. fruit
B. 1. true   2. false   3. false
C. Answers will vary—e.g., People
plant seeds. People feed seeds to
animals. People throw seeds on
the ground when they finish
eating.

Big Idea 1: Week 2 • Day 4
A. 1. sterile   2. mutation
B. Answers will vary.

Seedless fruit that you like to eat	Fruit that you wish didn't have seeds
Answers will vary—grapes, blueberries, watermelons, oranges, pineapple	Answers will vary—cherries, raspberries, apples, mangoes, strawberries

Big Idea 1: Week 2 • Day 5
A. 1. mutation   4. sterile
    2. pollination   5. Pollen,
    3. angiosperms   ovary
B. 4, 1, 5, 2, 3
C. Answers will vary—e.g.,
Angiosperms have flowers and
make seeds.

Big Idea 1: Week 3 • Day 1
A. proboscis, nectar
B. 1. allows the bee to get
      nectar that is hard to reach
    2. allows the bee to collect
      pollen easily

Big Idea 1: Week 3 • Day 2
A. Answers will vary—e.g., Worker
bees build the honeycomb
with wax from their glands.
Worker bees mold the honeycomb
with their mouths and feet.
B. 3, 1, 4, 2

Big Idea 1: Week 3 • Day 3
A. Answers will vary—e.g.,
The honeybee is smaller.
The bumblebee is larger. Both
have wings and six legs. The
bumblebee has a fatter back end.
The bumblebee has more hair.
B.

	Honeybee	Bumblebee
Pollinates flowers	✓	✓
Drinks nectar from flowers	✓	✓
Produces large amounts of honey	✓	
Creates honeycomb filled with honey	✓	
Often dies in the winter		✓
Depends on flowers for survival	✓	✓

Big Idea 1: Week 3 • Day 4
A. b, a, c
TALK: Answers will vary.

Big Idea 1: Week 3 • Day 5
A. a, c, b
B. 4, 1, 5, 2, 6, 3
C. 1. Bees pollinate flowers.
    2. Bees pollinate crops.
    3. Bees make honey.
D. Answers will vary—e.g., Only
some bees make honey.
Honeybees make a lot of honey.

Big Idea 1: Week 4 • Day 1
A. 4, 1, 3, 2
B. Birds would hoard sunflower
seeds because seeds last longer
than worms do.
C. Animals in tropical places
wouldn't need to hoard food
because the plants grow all
year-round.

Big Idea 1: Week 4 • Day 2
A. Fat provides energy.
Body fat can be stored for
later use.
B. winter, food, fat, more, energy

Big Idea 1: Week 4 • Day 3
1. dormant   3. dormant
2. hibernating   4. hibernating

Big Idea 1: Week 4 • Day 4
A. Plants are still growing and
producing food in warmer places.
Animals are not hibernating
and so are easier to find and eat.
Water is available to drink
because lakes and ponds are
not frozen.
B. The wolves migrate, too.

Daily Science • EMC 5014 • © Evan-Moor Corp.

Big Idea 1: Week 4 • Day 5
A. 1. migrate   3. hoard
    2. dormant   4. hibernate
B. 1. true   3. true
    2. false   4. true
C.
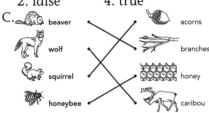

Big Idea 1: Week 5 • Unit Review 1
A. 1. A   2. B   3. D   4. A   5. D
B. Answers will vary—e.g.,
    1. Bees pollinate flowers.
    2. Plants provide food and
       shelter for animals.
    3. Animals eat fruit and
       distribute seeds.

Big Idea 1: Week 5 • Unit Review 2
A. 1. b   5. a   9. h
    2. i   6. j   10. d
    3. g   7. c
    4. e   8. f
B. habitat, nectar, pollen,
    pollinate, ovary

Big Idea 1: Week 5 • Unit Review 3
1. A   2. D   3. B

Big Idea 1: Week 5 • Unit Review 4
Answers will vary.

Big Idea 2: Week 1 • Day 1
A. 1. recycle nutrients
    2. enrich the soil
    3. get rid of the waste
B. 1. true   2. true   3. false
C. Answers will vary—e.g.,
    landfills, forests, in your home,
    in lakes

Big Idea 2: Week 1 • Day 2
A.

Size of bacteria	smallest decomposers
Where bacteria live	every ecosystem
How bacteria eat	absorb food

B. Answers will vary—e.g.,
    Bacteria live and grow better
    in warm places than they do
    in cold places.

Big Idea 2: Week 1 • Day 3
A. 1. fungus   2. Mold   3. absorb
B. Mushrooms are fungi. Fungi
    cannot make their own food
    like plants do.
C. C

Big Idea 2: Week 1 • Day 4
A. 1. true   2. false   3. false
B. 1. better   2. better   3. worse
TALK: Answers will vary—e.g.,
Gardeners can make sure the
compost is damp and warm and
keep chemicals out of the compost.

Big Idea 2: Week 1 • Day 5
A. bacteria, mold, fungus,
    decomposers, absorb
B. 1. false   2. true   3. false
C. Answers will vary—e.g.,
    When decomposers break
    down garbage, they produce
    substances that we smell as
    unpleasant odors.

Big Idea 2: Week 2 • Day 1
A. 1. true   4. true
    2. false   5. false
    3. false
B. Answers will vary—e.g.,
    Bacteria are decomposers.
    They probably break down your
    teeth and cause them to decay.

Big Idea 2: Week 2 • Day 2
A. bacteria, acid, dissolve
B.
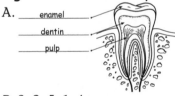

Big Idea 2: Week 2 • Day 3
A.
enamel
dentin
pulp
B. 3, 2, 5, 1, 4

Big Idea 2: Week 2 • Day 4
c, a, d, b
TALK: Answers will vary—e.g.,
Flossing removes food stuck
between your teeth that bacteria
could use to produce acid and
dissolve the enamel.

Big Idea 2: Week 2 • Day 5
A. plaque, acid, dissolve, cavity
B.
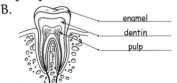
enamel
dentin
pulp

The *pulp* is the part of the tooth
that can become infected.

C. 1. false   3. true
    2. true   4. true

Big Idea 2: Week 3 • Day 1
A. 1. b   2. c   3. a
B. 3, 2, 1
C. 1. Both are microscopic.
    2. Both can be infectious.

Big Idea 2: Week 3 • Day 2
A. b, a, c
B. antibodies, immune system,
    viruses, reproduce

Big Idea 2: Week 3 • Day 3
1. They break down food we eat,
    which helps us absorb nutrients.
2. Antibiotics could kill the good
    bacteria we need to stay healthy.
3. They will get new bacteria to
    replace the bacteria that may
    be destroyed in their digestive
    system.

Big Idea 2: Week 3 • Day 4
A. 1. Some bacteria break down
       oil or toxic substances.
    2. Bacteria could be used to
       convert garbage into energy.
B. Answers will vary—e.g., The
    scientist could put the bacteria
    on several different things,
    such as oil or trash, and study
    the bacteria for a certain
    amount of time to see if it
    breaks down any of those
    things.

Big Idea 2: Week 3 • Day 5
A. 1. d   2. c   3. b   4. a   5. e
B. 1. true   3. false   5. false
    2. true   4. true   6. true
C. Answers will vary—e.g., If a
    person coughs or sneezes, he
    or she can spread viruses or
    bacteria through the air. If
    another person breathes in
    the virus or bacteria, that
    person might become ill.

Big Idea 2: Week 4 • Day 1
A. 1. microorganisms
    2. nutrients
B. leaking water pipe, locker room,
    garbage can

Big Idea 2: Week 4 • Day 2
A. 1. true   2. true   3. false
B. 1. It is safe when the mold has
       been added to the food on
       purpose.
    2. Mold and bacteria that you
       cannot see may still be in
       the food.

Big Idea 2: *Week 4 • Day 3*
A. 3, 1, 4, 2
B. 1. the yeast is not warm enough
   to reproduce.
   2. it is full of gas.
   3. the yeast is killed.

Big Idea 2: *Week 4 • Day 4*
A. 1. antibiotic   3. antibiotic
   2. penicillin   4. penicillin
B. 1. D   2. B

Big Idea 2: *Week 4 • Day 5*
A. yeast, fungus, microorganisms,
   nutritious, antibiotic, penicillin
B. 1. true   4. false
   2. false   5. true
   3. true

Big Idea 2: *Week 5 • Unit Review 1*
A. 1. D   2. A   3. C   4. D   5. B
B. Answers will vary—e.g.,
   1. They break down garbage
      to get rid of it.
   2. They enrich the soil with
      nutrients.

Big Idea 2: *Week 5 • Unit Review 2*
1. j	7. s	13. f	19. l
2. v	8. h	14. b	20. a
3. q	9. r	15. u	21. i
4. d	10. g	16. c	22. k
5. n	11. p	17. e	
6. o	12. t	18. m	

Big Idea 2: *Week 5 • Unit Review 3*
1. 20–29 years old
2. more than 60 years old
3. 20–29 years old
4. Tooth decay is a smaller
   problem because the total
   percentage of people with
   cavities is decreasing.

Big Idea 2: *Week 5 • Unit Review 4*
Answers will vary.

Big Idea 3: *Week 1 • Day 1*
A. 1. C   2. A
B. 1. erosion   3. weathering
   2. weathering   4. erosion

Big Idea 3: *Week 1 • Day 2*
A. 1, 3, 4, 2
B. 1. Rocky Mountains
   2. channels in the ground
C. 1. uplifted   2. channels

Big Idea 3: *Week 1 • Day 3*
A. Water seeped into cracks in the
   rocks and froze in the winter.
   When the water froze, it
   expanded and pushed the
   rocks apart.
   Then the pull of gravity caused
   sections of the canyon wall to
   collapse, making the canyon
   wider.
B. 1. water   3. wind
   2. ice   4. gravity
TALK: Answers will vary.

Big Idea 3: *Week 1 • Day 4*
1. Flooding might prevent the
   saltcedar from growing too
   thick. The floodwater will also
   wash away some of the
   built-up salt.
2. Flooding will create sandbars
   for the fish to lay eggs.
   Flooding will also help the fish
   find food.

Big Idea 3: *Week 1 • Day 5*
A. 1. channels   4. weathering
   2. uplifted   5. ecosystems
   3. erosion   6. expanded
B. 1. B   2. C
C. Glen Canyon Dam blocked the
   Colorado River. This harmed
   the ecosystem.
   Now the dam occasionally
   releases lots of water to help
   the ecosystem.

Big Idea 3: *Week 2 • Day 1*
A. 1. must be cold year-round
   2. more snow must fall than
      melt
B. 1. true   3. false
   2. false   4. true

Big Idea 3: *Week 2 • Day 2*
1. Meltwater causes some glaciers
   to slide.
2. Gravity causes some glaciers
   to spread out.

Big Idea 3: *Week 2 • Day 3*
A.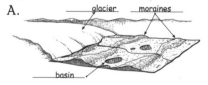
B. 1. basins   3. moraine
   2. moraines   4. basin

Big Idea 3: *Week 2 • Day 4*
1. 150 years   3. 1950–2000
2. 1900–1950
TALK: Answers will vary—e.g.,
sea levels would rise, the land
would change, the climate would
change, animal habitats would
change, etc.

Big Idea 3: *Week 2 • Day 5*
A. 1. moraines   4. meltwater
   2. glaciers   5. retreat
   3. basins
B. 1. false   3. true
   2. true   4. false
C. As layers of snow build up,
   the top layers add pressure to
   the bottom layers, turning
   them into dense ice.

Big Idea 3: *Week 3 • Day 1*
A.
B. 1. mantle, crust
   2. crust, mantle
C. Answers will vary—e.g.,
   The core would be densest
   because it is underneath the
   mantle and crust. The heaviest
   materials would sink to the
   core.

Big Idea 3: *Week 3 • Day 2*
A. 1. true   2. false   3. true
B. 1. They are both hot.
   2. Lava is liquid, but rock
      in the mantle is solid.
C. Answers will vary—e.g.,
   Magma is below Earth's crust,
   and lava is above it.

Big Idea 3: *Week 3 • Day 3*
A. Answers will vary—e.g.,
   Lava pours through vents in
   Earth's surface as lava flows.
   As the lava stacks up and
   cools, it creates rock that forms
   islands.
B. 1. false   2. false   3. false

Big Idea 3: *Week 3 • Day 4*
A. 1. debris   2. chamber
B. Answers will vary—e.g., The
   gases and magma are building
   up under the layers of rock,
   which makes the volcano bulge.

Big Idea 3: *Week 3 • Day 5*

A. 1. Magma, lava   3. vents
    2. core, mantle,   4. debris
      crust   5. chamber
B. 1. false   3. true
    2. true   4. true

Big Idea 3: *Week 4 • Day 1*

A. Answers will vary.
B. A
C. 1. true   2. false   3. true

Big Idea 3: *Week 4 • Day 2*

A. 1. north or northwest
    2. San Francisco, Los Angeles,
      San Diego
B. 1. plates   2. fault

Big Idea 3: *Week 4 • Day 3*

A. 1. moving apart
    2. sliding past
    3. colliding
B. 1. false   3. false
    2. false   4. true

Big Idea 3: *Week 4 • Day 4*

1. 1, 20   3. 4.0
2. 7.0   4. 144,434

Big Idea 3: *Week 4 • Day 5*

A. 1. boundaries   4. seismometer
    2. plates   5. magnitude
    3. fault
B. 1. sliding past each other
    2. moving apart
    3. coming together
C. Answers will vary—e.g.,
    1. Earth's plates float on
      the mantle.
    2. Earth's plates can cause
      earthquakes when they move.
    3. Earth's plates can create faults.

Big Idea 3: *Week 5 • Unit Review 1*

A. 1. B   2. C   3. B   4. A   5. B
B. Answers will vary—e.g.,
    Glaciers create moraines and
    basins; Erosion created the
    Grand Canyon; Plate movement
    causes earthquakes; Mountains
    form when plates collide.

Big Idea 3: *Week 5 • Unit Review 2*

DOWN   ACROSS
  1. plates   4. mantle
  2. erosion   6. uplifted
  3. meltwater   7. fault
  5. crust   10. weathering
  8. magma   12. lava
  9. moraines   13. basin
11. expanded   14. glacier

Big Idea 3: *Week 5 • Unit Review 3*

1. composite   4. composite
2. cinder   5. cinder
3. shield   6. composite

Big Idea 3: *Week 5 • Unit Review 4*

1. It scratched or tore the foil.
2. Water and sand were left
    behind. It would be called
    a moraine.
3. Glaciers can move rock, and
    these rocks can scratch other
    rocks.

Big Idea 4: *Week 1 • Day 1*

A. 1. when magma cools
    2. when water evaporates
B. 1. false   2. true   3. true

Big Idea 4: *Week 1 • Day 2*

A. 1. luster   2. streak   3. color
B. Geologists use many properties
    to identify minerals because
    some minerals show the same
    properties.

Big Idea 4: *Week 1 • Day 3*

A. 1. fracture   3. fracture
    2. cleavage   4. cleavage
B. They chose rocks with fracture,
    because they needed sharp edges.

Big Idea 4: *Week 1 • Day 4*

A. 1. 3   2. quartz   3. 4 and 5
B. Drills with diamonds in the
    tips can drill through any
    rock, because diamonds are
    the hardest minerals.

Big Idea 4: *Week 1 • Day 5*

A. 1. minerals   5. hardness
    2. fracture   6. luster
    3. cleavage   7. crystalline
    4. color, streak
B. 1. cleavage, fracture
    2. streak
    3. color, luster

Big Idea 4: *Week 2 • Day 1*

1. igneous   4. granite
2. crystals   5. microscope
3. pumice

Big Idea 4: *Week 2 • Day 2*

TALK: Answers will vary—e.g.,
As the landscape changes, rock
moves.

Big Idea 4: *Week 2 • Day 3*

A.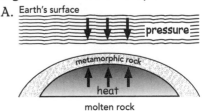

B. 1. Heat, pressure   3. melt
    2. metamorphic

Big Idea 4: *Week 2 • Day 4*

1. metamorphic   4. sedimentary
2. rock   5. magma
3. sediment

Big Idea 4: *Week 2 • Day 5*

A. 1. igneous   4. cement
    2. rock cycle   5. metamorphic
    3. Sedimentary, sediment
B. Answers will vary—e.g.,
    Igneous: contains crystals,
      formed from lava
    Metamorphic: can have
      swirls, formed from heat
      and pressure
    Sedimentary: made of sediment,
      formed from pressure
C. 1. erosion or weathering,
      cementing
    2. heat, pressure
    3. cooling

Big Idea 4: *Week 3 • Day 1*

Natural resources found above ground	Natural resources dug out of the ground
air	iron
water	limestone
plants, animals	oil, coal, and natural gas

Big Idea 4: *Week 3 • Day 2*

A. 4, 2, 3, 1
B. 1. true   2. false

Big Idea 4: *Week 3 • Day 3*

A.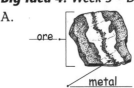

People often use machines
to *extract* natural resources
from the ground.
B. *mineral* is to *rock*
TALK: Answers will vary—e.g.,
They mined close to the surface,
because they didn't have the
tools to dig very deeply at first.
They used water, shovels, picks,
and—later—explosions to mine
for gold.

Big Idea 4: *Week 3 • Day 4*

A. 1. false   4. true
    2. true   5. false
    3. false

B. Answers will vary—e.g.,
By reducing, you use less
resources. By reusing, you
use a resource, such as a cup
or bag, over and over again so
that you don't need a new one.
By recycling, you reduce the
amount of new resources that
are needed.

Big Idea 4: *Week 3 • Day 5*

A. 1. natural resource, renewable
    2. fossil fuel, carbon
    3. Ore, metals
    4. conserve
    5. extract

B. Answers will vary—e.g.,

Fossil fuels I use:	How I use them:
1. oil	1. plastic bags and cups
2. natural gas	2. when I turn on the heater

Metals I use:	How I use them:
1. aluminum	1. my baseball bat
2. silver	2. my necklace

Big Idea 4: *Week 4 • Day 1*

A. 1. It can be very heavy.
    2. It can have an unusual shape.
    3. It can show signs of melting.
    4. It is very different from other
       rocks in the area.

B. A meteor is a streak of light
caused by an object burning
in Earth's atmosphere, but a
meteorite is an object from
space that hits Earth's surface.

Big Idea 4: *Week 4 • Day 2*

A. Scientists have difficulty
studying asteroids because
they are small and far away.

B. 1. true   2. false   3. true

Big Idea 4: *Week 4 • Day 3*

A. The Moon is made up of
igneous rock, because it is
cooled lava.

B. Similar: 1. contain similar
minerals and elements;
2. some rocks are made from
cooling lava
Different: 1. no weathering from
water or wind on the Moon;
2. fewer minerals in lunar rocks

Big Idea 4: *Week 4 • Day 4*

A. Mars has volcanoes, canyons,
and rocks very similar to those
on Earth.

B. Sedimentary rocks would
contain fossil remains, because
they would probably be
destroyed during the processes
that create igneous and
metamorphic rocks.

Big Idea 4: *Week 4 • Day 5*

A. meteor, meteorite, lunar,
maria, extraterrestrial, asteroid

B.

	Like Earth rocks	Different from Earth rocks
Lunar rocks	1. contain many of the same elements 2. some rocks made from lava	1. fewer minerals than Earth rocks 2. not changed by weathering
Mars rocks	1. contain hematite 2. weathering like Earth rock	1. unusual minerals not found on Earth

Big Idea 4: *Week 5 • Unit Review 1*

A. 1. C   2. B   3. C   4. D   5. A

B. Answers will vary—e.g.,
Streak—the mark a mineral
leaves behind; Color—the color
or colors a mineral appears to
be; Luster—the shininess of a
mineral; Cleavage/fracture—
how a mineral breaks when it
is struck; Hardness—how hard
a mineral is

Big Idea 4: *Week 5 • Unit Review 2*

1. t	5. k	9. e	13. c	17. g
2. m	6. q	10. o	14. b	18. s
3. a	7. d	11. l	15. i	19. n
4. j	8. f	12. h	16. p	20. r

Big Idea 4: *Week 5 • Unit Review 3*

1. calcite   4. quartz
2. quartz   5. apatite
3. graphite   6. hematite

Big Idea 4: *Week 5 • Unit Review 4*

1. The chalk in vinegar changed
more, because it started to
fizzle and dissolve.

2. It allows the vinegar to cover
more parts of the chalk and
work faster.

3. Because vinegar breaks down
limestone.

Big Idea 5: *Week 1 • Day 1*

A.

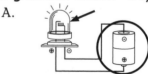

Big Idea 5: *Week 1 • Day 1* (continued)

B. Answers will vary—e.g., The
lever pops up to keep the toast
from burning. It breaks the
circuit.

Big Idea 5: *Week 1 • Day 2*

A. 1. true   3. false
    2. true   4. false

B. A resistor is not as good at
conducting electricity as a
conductor.

C. Answers will vary—e.g.,
Resistors helped toasters heat
up enough to toast bread.

Big Idea 5: *Week 1 • Day 3*

A. 3, 1, 2, 4

B. The length of time that the
filaments radiate heat will
change.

C. Answers will vary—e.g.,
1. sun   3. iron
2. electric stove

Big Idea 5: *Week 1 • Day 4*

A.

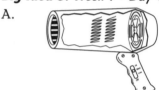

B. Answers will vary.

Big Idea 5: *Week 1 • Day 5*

A. 1. switch, circuit, electric
      current
    2. conductor, resistor
    3. filaments, radiate

B.

C. Answers will vary—e.g., They
need to move the iron to iron
out the wrinkles and not burn
the cloth.

Big Idea 5: *Week 2 • Day 1*

A.

B. 1. true   2. true   3. false
TALK: Answers will vary—e.g., The
lights last longer and are brighter.
This makes them easier to see.

Big Idea 5: *Week 2 • Day 2*

A.

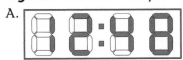

B. 17

C. Answers will vary—e.g., a computer screen

Big Idea 5: *Week 2 • Day 3*

A. Answers will vary—e.g., When the electrons flow through the LED, they get excited and release photons.

B. 2, 4, 1, 3, 5

Big Idea 5: *Week 2 • Day 4*

A. Answers will vary—e.g.,

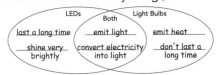

B. 1. LEDs convert more electricity into light than incandescent bulbs.
   2. LEDs are brighter than incandescent because they shine light in one direction.
   3. LEDs last much longer than incandescent bulbs.

Big Idea 5: *Week 2 • Day 5*

A. LEDs, display, electrons, photons

B.

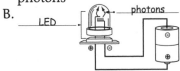

C. 1. heat: light
   2. circuits: photons
   3. less: more

Big Idea 5: *Week 3 • Day 1*

A. hearing aid, sound waves

B. 1. false   2. true   3. true

Big Idea 5: *Week 3 • Day 2*

A. 5, 3, 2, 1, 4

B. Answers will vary—e.g., Some sounds are louder than others, so it is necessary to be able to turn the volume on a hearing aid up or down.

Big Idea 5: *Week 3 • Day 3*

A.

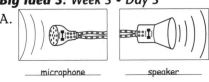

Big Idea 5: *Week 3 • Day 3*

B. 1. microphone   3. microphone
   2. speaker   4. amplifier

Big Idea 5: *Week 3 • Day 4*

A. 1. true   3. false
   2. true   4. false

B. Answers will vary—e.g.,
   1. stereo   3. loudspeaker
   2. headphones

Big Idea 5: *Week 3 • Day 5*

A. hearing aid, sound waves, microphone, amplifier, electromagnet, speaker

B.

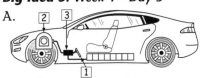

Answers will vary—e.g., Sound waves enter the microphone where they are turned into electric current. The current is sent to the amplifier, where it becomes stronger. It travels to the speaker, which turns the current back into sound waves and sends them into the middle ear.

Big Idea 5: *Week 4 • Day 1*

A. *electric car*

B. 1. electric motor, mechanical energy
   2. batteries
   3. the energy of motion or motion

Big Idea 5: *Week 4 • Day 2*

A. magnetic forces, electromagnet

B. 2, 5, 4, 1, 3

Big Idea 5: *Week 4 • Day 3*

A.

B. The coil receives the current. More current makes the rod spin faster, which makes the wheels spin faster.

Big Idea 5: *Week 4 • Day 4*

A.

Machine	Source of electricity (outlet or battery)	Which parts move?
Blender	outlet	blades
Clothes washer	outlet	inside basket
Electric toothbrush	battery	brush
Electric mixer	outlet	mixer blades
Remote-control car	battery	motor/wheel
Electric fan	outlet	fan blades

Big Idea 5: *Week 4 • Day 5*

A. 1. mechanical energy, electric motor
   2. controller
   3. electromagnet, magnetic force

B.

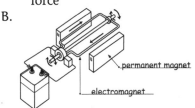

Big Idea 5: *Week 5 • Unit Review 1*

1. A   2. D   3. A   4. C   5. B   6. C

Big Idea 5: *Week 5 • Unit Review 2*

1. i   6. b   11. l   16. m
2. d   7. f   12. j   17. c
3. a   8. h   13. g
4. o   9. q   14. e
5. n   10. p   15. k

Big Idea 5: *Week 5 • Unit Review 3*

1. motion and light
2. light and sound
3. light and heat
4. light, motion, and sound
5. light and sound
6. sound
7. heat

Big Idea 5: *Week 5 • Unit Review 4*

1. The screw and magnet lifted up with it.
2. The screw and magnet spun around.
3. The wire is the electromagnet because it has a magnetic force created by electricity.

Big Idea 6: *Week 1 • Day 1*

A. *triangle* is to *shape*

B. 1. ramp   4. escalator
   2. slide   5. trail up a hill
   3. ladder

Big Idea 6: *Week 1 • Day 2*

A. Both people are doing the same amount of work.

B. 1. force   2. distance   3. work

Big Idea 6: *Week 1 • Day 3*

A. 1. Marco   2. Maria

B.

Answers will vary—e.g., You use more force because the ramp is shorter and steeper.

Big Idea 6: *Week 1 • Day 4*

A. Answers will vary—e.g.,
   1. restaurant   3. library
   2. post office   4. shopping mall

B. 1. ladder   2. slide

Big Idea 6: *Week 1 • Day 5*

A. work, inclined plane, simple machine, distance, force

B.

C. Answers will vary—e.g., Inclined planes make work easier by allowing a person to use less force over a greater distance.

Big Idea 6: *Week 2 • Day 1*

A.

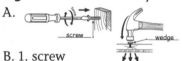

B. 1. screw
   2. wedge
   3. simple machines
   4. changes direction

Big Idea 6: *Week 2 • Day 2*

A. 1. dirt 2. cloth 3. food 4. wood
B. Answers will vary—e.g., A nail is a wedge that changes the direction of some of the force applied to it in order to push the wood out of its way.

Big Idea 6: *Week 2 • Day 3*

A.

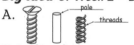

B. inclined plane
C. The screw will come out.

Big Idea 6: *Week 2 • Day 4*

A. Long, thick nails create more friction.
B. Answers will vary—e.g.,
   1. Both are simple machines.
   2. Both change the direction of the force applied to them.
C. Answers will vary—e.g.,
   1. A nail is a wedge, but a screw is a screw.
   2. A screw requires a circular force, but a nail does not.

Big Idea 6: *Week 2 • Day 5*

A. 1. wedge   3. screw
   2. threads 4. friction

B. 1. true 2. false 3. false 4. true
C.

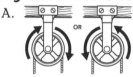

wedge   wedge   screw   screw   wedge

Big Idea 6: *Week 3 • Day 1*

A. 1. pulley   3. elevators
   2. wheel, groove
B. 1. true   2. true   3. false
TALK: Answers will vary—e.g., A pulley is like an inclined plane because it changes the amount of force needed to do work. It is like a screw because it changes the direction of the force applied to it.

Big Idea 6: *Week 3 • Day 2*

A.

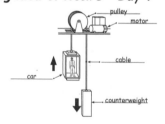

B. 1. true   2. false   3. false
C. 1. makes it easier to lift the flag high
   2. makes it easier to lower the bucket to a place people can safely go

Big Idea 6: *Week 3 • Day 3*

Answers will vary—e.g.,
1. It allows you to do work with less force.
2. Add more movable pulleys.
3. to reduce the amount of force needed to move something

Big Idea 6: *Week 3 • Day 4*

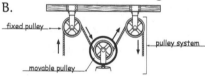

Big Idea 6: *Week 3 • Day 5*

A. 1. counterweight
   2. movable
   3. fixed
   4. mechanical advantage
B.

Big Idea 6: *Week 4 • Day 1*

1. the lever, the container, and the wheel and axle
2. the lever and the wheel and axle

TALK: Answers will vary—e.g., People who need to move heavy loads use wheelbarrows. They are not used as much today because we have other machines to help us move heavy loads.

Big Idea 6: *Week 4 • Day 2*

A. Answers will vary—e.g., When you push down or pull up the lever, it raises or lowers the load.
B. Answers will vary—e.g.,
   1. door handle   3. pole vault
   2. pliers   4. chopsticks

Big Idea 6: *Week 4 • Day 3*

A.

B. 1. true   2. false
C. 1. wheel 2. axle 3. wheel 4. axle

Big Idea 6: *Week 4 • Day 4*

A. 1. ___wedge___ 2. ___lever___ 3. ___lever___
   ___lever___   ___wedge___   ___wheel and axle___
   or wheel and axle
B. *lever* is to *scissors*

Big Idea 6: *Week 4 • Day 5*

A. 1. fulcrum   2. lever
   3. compound machine
   4. wheel and axle
B. 1. false 2. true 3. true 4. false
C. Answers will vary.

Big Idea 6: *Week 5 • Unit Review 1*

1. B 2. C 3. B 4. A 5. B 6. C

Big Idea 6: *Week 5 • Unit Review 2*

ACROSS   **DOWN**
1. wedge   1. wheel and axle
4. screw   2. fixed pulley
7. compound   3. friction
   machine   4. simple machine
9. pulley   5. work
10. distance   6. lever
11. force   8. fulcrum

Big Idea 6: *Week 5 • Unit Review 3*

can opener: wedge, lever, wheel and axle
fishing pole: lever, wheel and axle
drill: screw, wheel and axle
scissors: wedge, lever
shovel: wedge, lever
bicycle: wheel and axle, lever

Big Idea 6: *Week 5 • Unit Review 4*

Answers will vary.